The Batsford Embroidery Course

The Batsford Embroidery Course

R. Anne Williams

B. T. Batsford Ltd

First published 1991

ISBN 0 7134 6479 8

Typeset by Keyspools Ltd, Golborne, Lancs.
and printed in Hong Kong

for the Publishers
B. T. Batsford Ltd
4 Fitzhardinge Street
London W1H 0AH

Frontispiece
The Toucans Nina Humphries

Contents

Foreword

People have often said to me, 'If only there were classes that I could attend, but I live too far away and I do want to start to embroider. Where can I obtain information that would enable me to learn about design related to emboidery, where would I look to find out about fabrics, threads and stitches? What books are available on ways of working and the different types of embroidery?'

'How would I find out about all those things and other details that would be useful and necessary if I could start on my own?'

Anne Williams' book is an answer to the many questions that are asked, and has been written to help such would-be embroiderers. It should be invaluable to those who are really keen to learn but have little idea on where and how to find the information they require. She has done an enormous amount of research, resulting in a great deal of knowledge not often found in one volume. The very extensive bibliography makes this book really valuable to all embroiderers however much they know. For the beginner, Anne suggests ways in which design, the knowledge of types of embroidery and of the details of techniques may be researched advantageously.

Anyone interested in embroidery will find many useful 'wrinkles' that have been learnt through experience and I congratulate Anne on putting together such a book.

CONSTANCE HOWARD MBE, ARCA, ATD, FSDC
(*President of the West Country Embroiderers 1988–9*)
September 1989

Preface

Anne Williams successfully pioneered her particular method of distance learning for the City and Guilds of London Institute Embroidery examination, and has made participation possible for students living in areas where no such course is available. She now sets out the requirements and disciplines needed for the student to embark on a well prepared distance-learning course.

Having explained the course, she then provides a most comprehensive list of tools and materials required. Chapter by chapter she takes the student through the stages of the course, giving clear help and instruction for tackling each stage.

In a period of increasing interest, ability and challenge in embroidery as both a craft and an art form, this book will surely encourage more people to study the subject seriously and to develop their own preferences and aptitudes from the enormous range of variations existing, while at the same time encouraging students to produce work to the best of their abilities.

BILLIE CARR-GOMM
Chairman of The West Country Embroiderers 1984–5

Introduction

Distance learning has become an integral part of modern teaching methods. This book was originally designed for The West Country Embroiderers' students in south-west England who were preparing for the City and Guilds of London Institute Examinations in Embroidery. It will enable the interested embroiderer with sufficient motivation and self-discipline to cover a full course in embroidery as we know it in the United Kingdom. The West Country Embroiderers' was the first non-institutional organization to be granted the status of an 'Examination Centre' by the City and Guilds of London Institute.

The guidance gained from face-to-face tutorials and the facilities provided by a College of Further Education, as well as the encouragement of working with like-minded students, are luxuries not by any means open to all. It is hoped that this book will be useful to those who work at home in their own time without necessarily wishing to take examinations and to those who, for whatever reason, are unable to attend a course at a local institution. Such courses often fail because an insufficient number of students are available to support the cost of venue and tutor. Neither of these difficulties has hampered the WCE students, whose members are restricted only by their tutor's facilities for offering regular tutorials.

A full Bibliography is offered as it is an essential part of the course that students use library facilities to do research in their chosen fields of study. Far from acting as a brake on our students, this emphasis on going out to look for knowledge has proved to be the perfect counterpoint to the distance-learning concept, and provides a first-class opportunity for students to stretch their minds and legs, thus avoiding the occasional ennui of the lone worker.

I should like to thank those Student Members of the WCE who, through their enthusiasms and perseverance, 'proved' the course. Their excellent results over the years and the enquiries from various parts of Britain and other countries to join the course led to this attempt to provide a guide for serious embroiderers, and I would like to wish all students who may use this book a very happy and rewarding experience.

R. ANNE WILLIAMS
Walditch, 1990

Treleigh altar frontal Sereta Thompson.

Acknowledgment

The author wishes to thank the following for their help and encouragement:

The membership of The West Country Embroiderers, particularly the students of the WCE 'City and Guilds' course over the last ten years, to whom this book is dedicated; all the students whose work appears in this book and those who allowed their work to be photographed although there was not space for it to be included; Mrs Jenny Best for illustrations; Martin Dickson for advice; Euan Williams for chapter 24 'Recording your embroidery', his patient photography of students' work, his help in preparing the Bibliography and for sorting out and typing various versions of the script, correcting errors and making many helpful suggestions; Arnold and Betty Vos for correcting the proofs; the Churchwardens of St Mary's, Netherbury, for permission to photograph their altar frontal; the Vicar and Churchwardens of St Stephen's Church, Treleigh, Cornwall for permission to photograph the Altar Frontal by Sereta Thompson; the Churchwardens of St Mary's Church, Walditch, for permission to photograph the burse and veil; the City and Guilds of London Institute for examining our students and then granting the West Country Embroiderers the status of a 'Centre'; and to the following shops for lending items for photography: The Fabric Shop, Honiton, Devon for the loan of embroidery threads; Frank Herring and Sons, Dorchester, Dorset, for the loan of graphics and mounting tools; Livingstone Textiles, Bridport, Dorset, for the loan of fabric swatches; Creativity Needlecrafts, London, for the loan of materials for the jacket picture; to the Dorset County Library, Dorchester, reference and requests librarians for advice, and the use of their wide-ranging facilities when preparing the Bibliography.

There are many people – members of the Royal School of Needlework, members of the Embroiderers' Guild, members of the West Country Embroiderers, and others – whose contributions are not acknowledged here and who may not even be aware of having contributed – to them, also, I owe a debt of thanks; and in particular to all those who have, over the years, passed on their knowledge, insights and enthusiasm.

Lastly, my thanks to my family, Simon and Helen, Alastair and Emma, and Euan – all of whom encouraged me to persevere.

1
How to use this book

This book provides the groundwork and references necessary to complete a do-it-yourself or a more formal distance-learning course in British embroidery. Some of the work and information may already be familiar to the reader; nevertheless the book is intended to take the complete beginner from the first use of the needle and thread on fabric through the difficulties of design and ultimately to creating personally satisfying pieces of work. The book continues with a brief treatment of other embroidery traditions as they are interwoven with English embroidery.

I hope that readers will always think of themselves as 'designer-embroiderers' and not as 'stitchers'. There is a difference.

The Bibliography is essential and you should use library facilities to support your studies. This emphasis on seeking knowledge is essential to distance-learning, since it stretches your mind and imagination beyond the simple and the homely.

In a book of this nature it really is necessary to go through systematically step-by-step in the order provided; so, having obtained the equipment, begin with stitches and progress to techniques. While doing this practical work, read and make notes from all the books you can lay your hands on, noting where they do not agree and where familiar embroidery stitches often have different names. For example, the USA is now publishing and returning to England books with techniques that originated in Europe, which have altered as they have passed into the traditions of other countries.

Books on embroidery are being published at a great rate, and while it is necessary to be aware of them, owning and reading all of them closely is not essential. You should try to acquire practice in knowing which books will give you the greatest help. You really need to discriminate between basic knowledge and irrelevant facts. It is easy to waste time unless the habit of self-discipline is developed, particularly in distance learning.

Tools and materials

First, you will want to collect some tools. You may already have many of those listed below, but they are mentioned as necessary to the successful pursuit of your goal.

Embroidery tools

Tools are an important and necessary possession for the serious embroiderer and are mostly best acquired individually. The made-up packages sold at inflated prices often prove inadequate.

Frames

It really is necessary to use a frame. There are several types which have different uses, but if you can only manage to buy one frame, an adjustable slate frame will serve for most purposes except machine embroidery. Other types are:
- round or tambour frame
- slate or picture frame
- adjustable frames using pegs or screws (floor or free-standing)

You will find advice on how to dress and use a frame in chapter 2.

Storage

An efficient way to keep these items is in a fisherman's accessory box, which folds out into a multitude of small compartments and is generally rust-free.

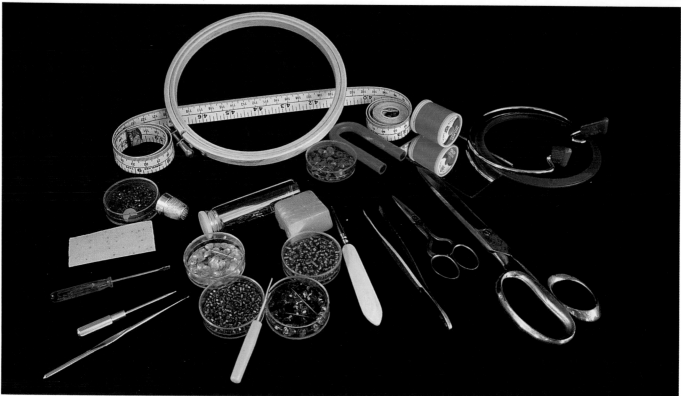

Pins, scissors, tools, etc.

Needles
You will need a selection of:
- chenille
- circular
- shorts
- tapestry
- bead

Also an emery cushion to keep them in condition and a needle threader to help you with the finer needles.

Scissors
- Large cutting-out scissors
- medium general-purpose scissors
- small fine-pointed embroidery scissors (these must all be made of good steel which can be sharpened regularly and reset – never use them for cutting paper, card or hair!)
- scissors for cutting paper and card
- an old pair of curved nail scissors for cutting metal threads and curves

Pins
- A box of good quality wedding-veil pins (these do not rust and are long and fine gauge, but note that a magnet will not pick them up)
- box of bead-top pins

Miscellaneous tools
- 'Quikunpic'
- small magnet
- tape measure
- two thimbles
- crochet hook
- stiletto and tweezers
- bodkin for threading tape, ribbon and so on
- pin-board
- rings and a cloth binder to store threads
- magnifying glass on a stand (as used by stamp collectors and weavers)
- adjustable reading lamp (some have a magnifying glass, which can be useful)

Sewing machine
Preferably with a swing needle

Design tools
Drawing tools:
- compass
- rulers (transparent plastic (short and long) and 'Tee' square)
- set square
- protractor
- steel ruler
- drawing board and pins
- selection of good quality pencils
- rubber eraser and 'putty' rubber eraser

- drafting pen with interchangeable nibs
- inks

Adhesives
- Tapes:
  masking tape
  double-sided 'Sellotape'
- Glues:
  PVA glue ('school glue')
  'UHU' (caution: this is inclined to stain fabrics)
  glue stick (e.g. 'Pritt')

Paints
- Each type of paint in the three primary hues – red, yellow and blue – plus white and black. (Tubes are the most economical.) Poster paints do not blend colours well and will require added 'violet'.

Felt-tip pens

Dyes and dye paints
(See chapter 7 for details)

Paper and binders
- Ring binders and transparent folders to store your work, plus a punch to fit rings
- stapler
- A4 paper (lined and plain)
- A4 cartridge paper
- graph paper
- squared paper
- printed geometric pattern paper
- tracing paper
- some newspaper colour supplement pages
- dressmaker's carbon paper and tracing wheel
- adhesive coloured paper
- cardboard (thin)

Design tools

Mounting tools
Cutting tools
- 'Stanley' knife and cutting board
- scalpel

Mounting tools
- Sheet of chipboard to protect your table
- steel straightedge
- carpenter's set-square
- carpenter's chisel-edge pencil
- specialist cutter to cut mounting card
- frame cutting guide

Mounting materials
- Mounting card (suitable for lacing heavy fabric without buckling)
- thin padding, such as flock paper, or fine flannel (all embroideries are enhanced by using a thin interlining over the card)
- suitable coloured card for mounting surrounds
- other padding material
- hanging rings
- lacing cord

2
Frames, fabrics and threads

Round or tambour frame

For small pieces the hand-held frame is useful, but there is a mounted kind which is fixed to a table and is flexible. The 'Fanny' frame is a tambour frame which is anchored by sitting on it.

With round frames the inner ring must be bound with tape to prevent slipping. Make certain that the grain of the material is straight within the frame. Placing the outer ring on the table, first cover it with some tissue or thin cloth, then with the fabric to which the design has already been transferred, and then with any backing needed. Finally, press the tape-bound inner ring into place. The ring is usually tightened by a thumb screw and the fabric should be drum-tight. The paper can be torn back to reach the design and will prevent the tell-tale ring of grime which appears however careful one is.

A quilting frame is a very large ring frame. Prepare as above, but the backing fabric should be drum-tight while the top fabric, which carries the design, should be tacked to the lower fabric and allowance made to ease the top fabric as the quilting takes up the slack.

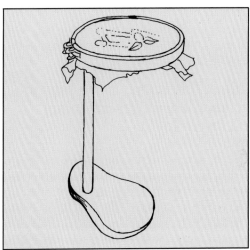

Figure 2
Fanny frame

Figure 3
Tambour frame with clamp

The slate or picture frame

This is also bound and the fabric pinned or stapled all around the frame. Again, the fabric must be straight on the grain: staple the centre of each side first and move out to the corners

Figure 1
Tambour frame

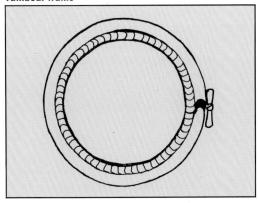

Figure 4
Slate frame

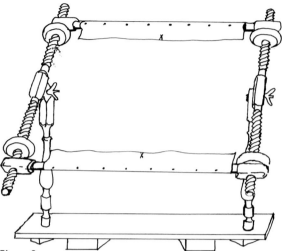

Figure 6
Table stand frame

keeping the grain straight (drawing pins may be used). Such frames can be clamped to the table with a 'G' clamp.

Adjustable frames using pegs or screw (floor or free-standing)

The fabric must be tacked to the webbing on the top and bottom rollers. Note that the fabric must be straight to the grain. Mark the centre of the edge of the webbing and the centre edge of the fabric with tacking stitches. Match the two centre tacks of the fabric and the webbing and tack both together beginning at the centre edges. Work outwards to left and right. The side of the fabric is laced to the side of the frame. Before lacing, fold the fabric edge over a taut reinforcing string – attached to the top and bottom rods of the frame – and lace round this edge. This will take strain and prevent the fabric being spoilt.

A long piece of work can be rolled over these

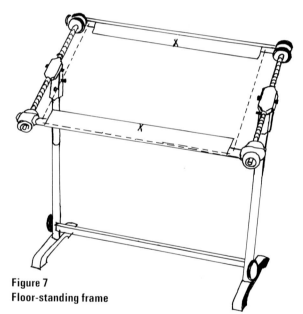

Figure 7
Floor-standing frame

Figure 5
Slate frame adjustable by pegs

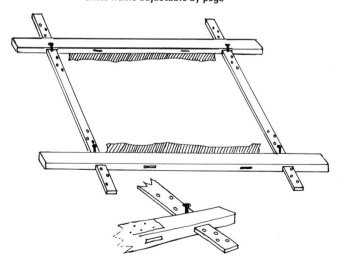

rods to facilitate working, using a piece of old fabric or acid-free tissue paper – layered to prevent damage. The sides must be re-laced to the frame after being wound on.

Canvas, being a stiff fabric, is better mounted on a frame of this kind – bind the raw edges with masking tape. Where delicate fabrics are used, the frame is first dressed as above with a fine but firm fabric – calico, for example. The delicate fabric is then tacked to the background with a long and short stitch or a herringbone stitch, care being taken to align the grain of the fabric without any ruckles.

Fabric swatches

This type of frame can be finely adjusted, giving the fabric a firm and almost drum-tight tension.

These frames are easily the most versatile to use, although sadly they are also the most expensive.

Fabrics and threads

Natural and synthetic fibres

Keep a rag bag and collect a wide selection of fabrics and threads such as natural cotton, wool, silk and leather and the man-made fibres such as rayon, nylon and polyester; also include string, raffia and any threads you may spin for yourself.

The traditional fabrics of linen, silk, cotton and wool, remain the most pleasant fabrics to work with. However, there is a bewildering number of fabrics, each of which needs to be explored and experimented with. Such fabrics and threads will suggest fresh specialized techniques to enhance their qualities, and especially to bring out their often intriguing textures.

You should make a serious study of these. Divide them into woven, felted and chemically bonded for fabrics; and spun, extruded, stretched and fibrillated, and air-spun for threads. There are many combinations of these and they need to be explored. Use a modern encyclopaedia and look for them under the appropriate manufacturing techniques for yarns and fabrics.

Make a collection of 5×5 cm $(2 \times 2$ in) squares and sort them into their correct groups, such as cellulose-based (cotton, linen, rayon) protein-based (such as wool, hair, and so on) and other man-made chemical bases such as polypropylene (garden and binder twine), nylon (stockings and monofilament sewing thread). Then match as many trade names to these as you can, such as Terylene (ICI) Celanese (British Celanese) and so forth. List beside each sample the uses to which you would put it and also the washing or cleaning care label you would give it. In this way you will come to understand the man-made fabrics and how to use them.

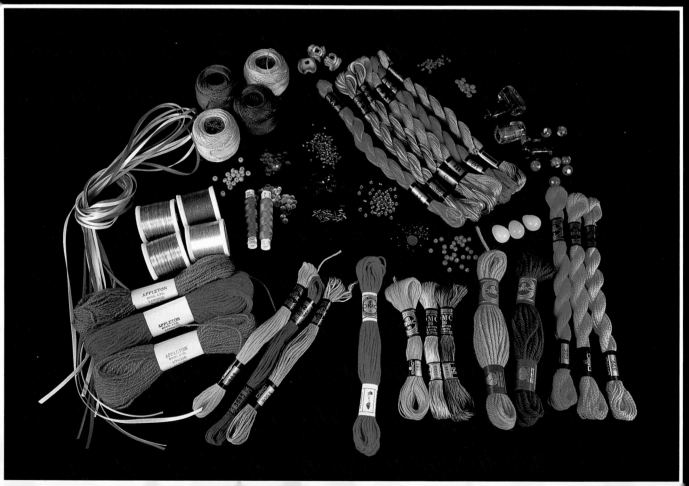

Vanishing muslin

The soluble fabric known as 'vanishing muslin' is most useful to the machine embroiderer who wishes to create a lace-like effect. It is available in three types: one vanishes with the application of heat with an iron, one by soaking in hot water, and the third by soaking in cold. Acetone will dissolve simple rayon, and this method may also be used, even if it is a little hazardous: strict safety precautions should be observed. The use of these techniques will be discussed later under 'Machine Embroidery'.

Metal threads

These are made in a variety of metals and textures – gold, silver, copper and aluminium anodised in various colours, as well as metallised plastic film 'yarns' such as 'Lurex'. Traditional metal threads consist of a very thin strip of metal foil mounted on paper and wrapped around a silk cord. Today the metal is often artificial and silk cord has modern substitutes.

Jewel case Jeanette Morton

Opposite: fabrics and threads

3

Design basics

Designing with a pencil

For some people, the whole prospect of designing something is fraught with the possibility of at best a mess, and at worst, failure; these exercises will help you to avoid both fates. At the back of this book are sheets of working diagrams. Each is numbered to match a selection of the exercises in the following chapters. Keep this set of outlines intact and make copies of them to work with.

Pencil exercises

1. Make two ladder-shaped rectangles $26 \times 6\,cm$ $(10\frac{1}{4} \times 2\frac{1}{4}\,in)$ on good drawing paper. Now draw twelve lines across each at 2 cm intervals. This will make thirteen spaces.

With a soft pencil (2B) shade from white through grey to jet black. Now reverse and go black to white – see below (an easy way to obtain clear edges is to place a ruler against the straight and work to the edge). The shading on the seventh space should be the same either way.

2. Take a large A2 $(60 \times 40\,cm/23\frac{1}{2} \times 15\frac{3}{4}\,in)$ sheet of firm paper and along the longest side mark out five columns. Place it on a firm floor, kneel down and, with an easy flowing movement of your arm, let the pencil draw out a curving line in wide sweeps across all the columns, starting in the top left-hand side of column one. Then do the same thing with straight, jagged, and looped lines.

Following one of these lines, 'dot' along its

Figure 8
Pencil exercise – exercise 1

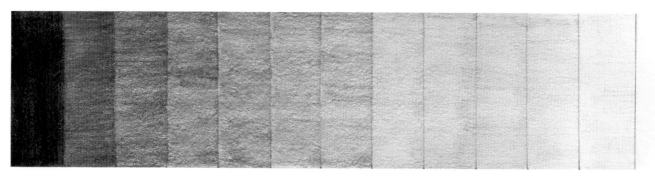

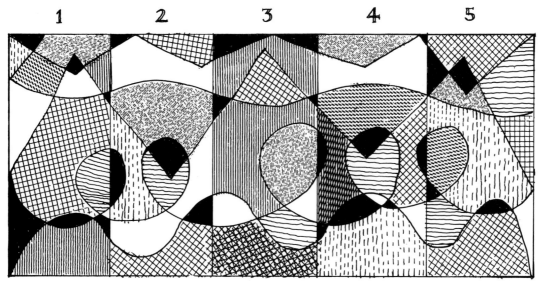

Figure 9
Floor exercise – exercise 2

length, then 'dot-dash' on a second, and 'dash' along the length of a third.

Now you will have a number of areas of different volumes; using a short ruler try filling these areas with lines – some close, some spaced and some far apart. They can also be cross-hatched at various angles and widths. This will gradually build up a series of shapes and patterns which should enable you to see how the darkest object appears to be in the foreground and the lightest in the background.

The next two exercises will show the differences between straight and curved lines.
3. Make two rectangles 17×8 cm ($6\frac{3}{4} \times 3\frac{1}{8}$ in). Using a set square, divide one with straight lines, and using a pair of compasses divide the second with curves. As these shapes

appear – don't overdo the divisions – make a note of what they call to mind. Fill one with pencil shading and the other with patterns.
4. Make a square 16×24 cm ($6\frac{1}{4} \times 9\frac{1}{2}$ in) and divide it into a grid 4×4 cm ($1\frac{1}{2} \times 1\frac{1}{2}$ in). With some firm card and a Stanley knife make one sharp and exact 4 cm square window. Keep the square cut-out.

Armed with a 2B pencil or a stick of cobbler's wax, go outside and around the house and fill the squares with a wide variety of rubbings. Holding the window over each square will help to keep it distinct. Make as many rubbings as you please – they will all be interesting and useful. None of these exercises requires drawing in the accepted sense.

On some of these grids, using your putty rubber, very gently remove parts of the rubbing to make a further variety of designs. You

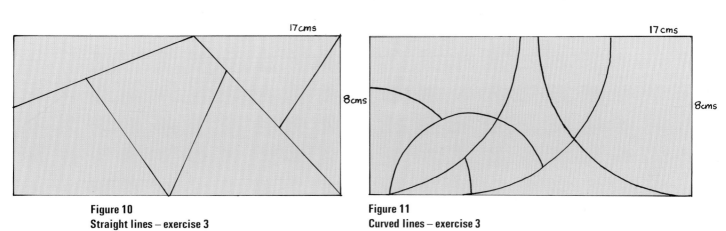

Figure 10
Straight lines – exercise 3

Figure 11
Curved lines – exercise 3

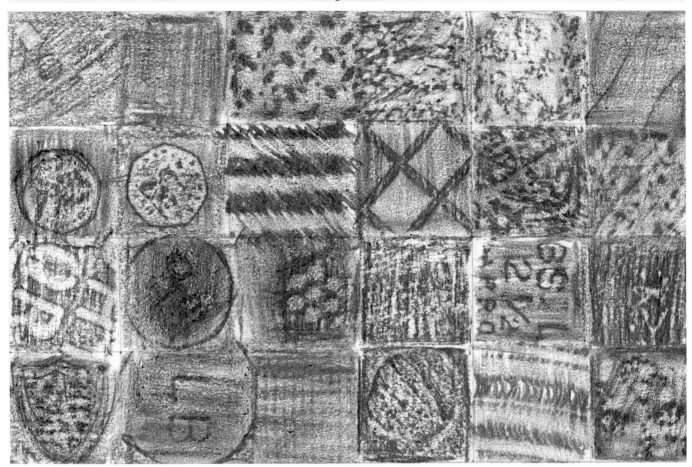

Figure 12
Rubbings – exercise 4

could also make a ragged-edged window by tearing a circle out of a piece of firm paper and using it as a mask either for the cobbler's wax or for the rubber.

Through these exercises you will get a feel for changing shapes. The design that builds up through the contrasts helps you to see what you look at and to appreciate the spaces in between which are also a part of the design; only accuracy and care are needed, not the ability to draw; so, you see, there is no mystery. Play with these ideas, shapes and patterns until you begin to see new patterns and familiar shapes emerging. It may be useful to half close your eyes or to take off your spectacles for a while.

5. Now make another grid measuring 16×16 cm ($6\frac{1}{4} \times 6\frac{1}{4}$ in) and divide it into sixteen 4 cm ($1\frac{1}{2}$ in) squares. Find some large plain newspaper headline letters, such as those used by the tabloid press. The letters must be straight.

Choose six with very different shapes, such as 'U' 'W' 'N' 'P' 'E' and 'S'. Trace these shapes. Using the six letters, place each in any position, not necessarily using the whole of the letter. In the first square, for example, trace in 'N', in the next 'N' and 'S', and so on until all six squares are filled. Each successive square is filled with an extra letter, so that square six has all the letters in it. Then with your 2B pencil shade in each letter, commencing with the first in the lightest tone and ending with the last in the darkest. You can trace these letters by reversing the tracing paper.

Adapting ready-made shapes

On an A4 sheet of paper, draw around a selection of articles such as keys, springs, clock parts, paperclips, scissors, spoons and so on, turning them this way and that, overlapping them, and so forth.

Keep these exercises, because you will be transferring the same ideas into colour and ultimately into fabric and thread.

Not all of these exercises are illustrated here; many are left to the reader's imagination and ingenuity.

Figure 13
Random letters – exercise 5

The sketching daybook

When you have tackled these exercises in pencil, try to draw in a sketchbook for at least twenty minutes every day. It does not matter whether your talents are good or indifferent; everyone can draw, including you. A list of subjects is included below and you should go through them, devoting one week to each and drawing every possible aspect of it that you can find. After drawing all the subjects, which will take you about a year, you will have a very good grounding in this essential discipline.

Do not worry if your early efforts are not very accurate – remember that the basis of design is to observe what you are looking at. You will soon surprise yourself and acquire this facility.

List of subjects for 20 minutes-a-day sketches

Trees
Pot plants
Doors
Windows
Ironwork
Sea shore and rivers
Animals, fur and skin
Birds and feathers
Street furniture
House furniture
Machinery
Trains
Wheels
Gates
Roofs
Chimneys

Hedges, railings
    and barriers
Woodcarvings
Fossils, fungi
    and stains
Insects
Water and
    reflections
Garden furniture
Tools – kitchen,
    garden and
    workshop
Ships
Vehicles
Clouds

4
Colour basics

The following exercises are deliberately neat and precise, which is good practice for the absolute requirement that you learn to see what you are looking at. It is necessary to maintain a strong measure of self-discipline in neatness. Slovenly work is simply not acceptable to the embroiderer.

In embroidery, as in other forms of the creative arts, colour is an essential element. The technical term for colour is 'hue'. Without an understanding of colour, it is not easy to use this important element successfully in your designs. This is not the place to study the subject except as it relates to your own work and for this reason much has been excluded. Should you wish to study it further, some books on the subject are listed in the Bibliography.

The first exercises are to be carried out in a pigment, preferably poster, gouache, or acrylic, as these give a bright, clean result. A little practice may be needed beforehand.

Read Chapter IV of 'Art School', edited by Colin Saxton, for an excellent treatment of colour – see Bibliography, page 125.

Exercises

6. Achromatic scale – black and white
Make two ladder-shaped rectangles $26 \times 4 \times 2$ cm ($10\frac{1}{4} \times 1\frac{1}{2} \times \frac{3}{4}$ in) of thirteen spaces on white cartridge paper; paint from white to black on one ladder and black to white on the other – see below. Each space should be consistently graded. Black and white cannot be said to have any colour, but this scale gives varying tones of grey.

7. Monochrome
Using the same ladder outline as the achromatic scale, but with only eleven spaces, take one of the primary hues and paint it in the centre space of the ladder. Add white to the left and black to the right, and then reverse the series in the second ladder.

8. Neutral tone
Using the 'neutral' diagram in the appendix, paint blue in the left-hand outer space and orange in the right-hand outer space, adding black increasingly to each colour so that they meet at the centre with the same tone, which will be a thoroughly nasty brown mess! Now do the same sort of thing up and down,

Figure 14
Achromatic – exercise 6

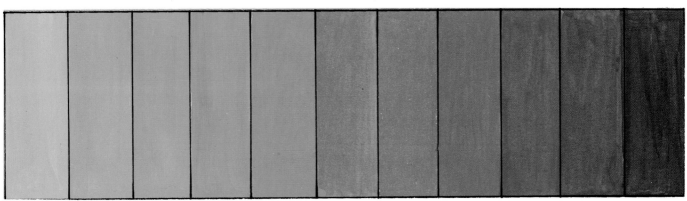

Figure 15
Monochrome – exercise 7

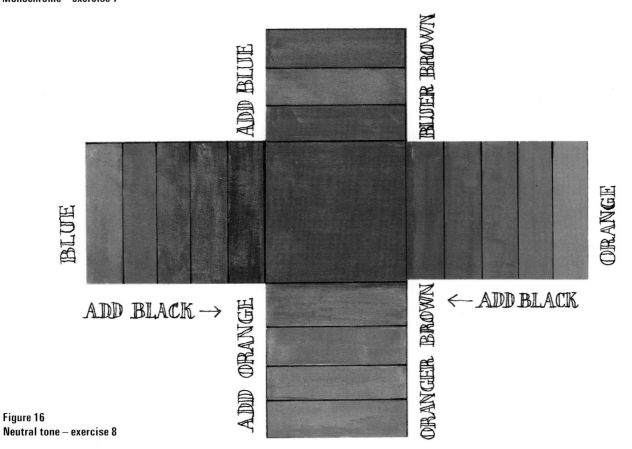

Figure 16
Neutral tone – exercise 8

starting with the messy brown and adding orange or blue.

9. Primary hues

Choose one of the three primary hues – red, yellow or blue. Make a grid eleven sections across and six sections down. In the central column place the brightest hue (i.e. the reddest red, the yellowest yellow, and the bluest blue). Working to the left, add a little more white each time, giving a paler, luminous tone. To the right, add black as above, and this will give a darker, sombre tone. Then work down the grid, converting each paler red to the (relatively) darkest red and each darker red to the (relatively) palest.

Figure 17
Primary hues – exercise 9. This chart is wrong; why?

What is wrong with figure 17? The top row is fair, as is the second row to the left. Write in each pro-forma grid rectangle your criticism. Never try to re-colour a faulty rectangle, do the job again – but keep your mistakes: this might have been a quilt design.

10. Colour wheels

This colour wheel shows primary, secondary and further hues. Yet more subdivisions will give even greater variety. You could experiment by taking a primary of secondary hue and using white/black to produce a gradation of hues equal to all the manufactured colours in a commercial paint box; the red and blue are the least consistent and need additions of black/white to make a violet. If you are using poster paints, it is necessary to buy 'violet' because the clear violet needed cannot be mixed from red and blue; this is simpler with watercolours.

The wax crayon colouring in Fig 19 shows how difficult it is to mix colours accurately this way. The wax crayon reproduction gives a sense of how colours are built up in fabric with thread, so do one yourself for practice.

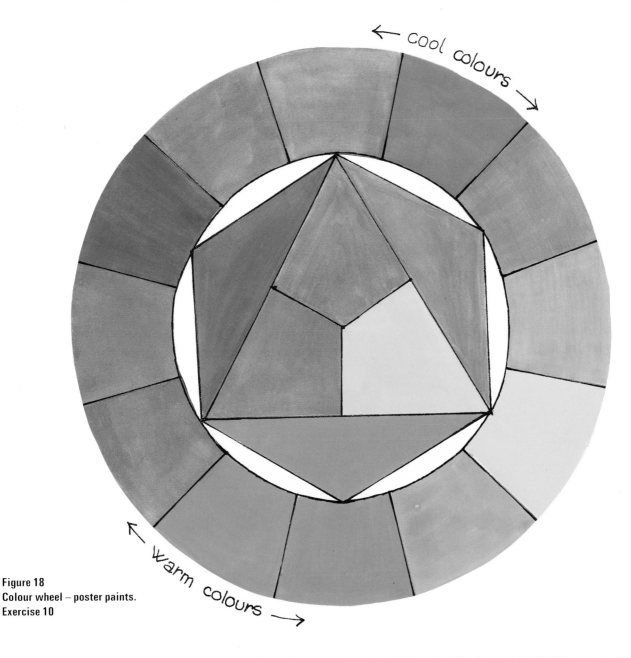

Figure 18
Colour wheel – poster paints.
Exercise 10

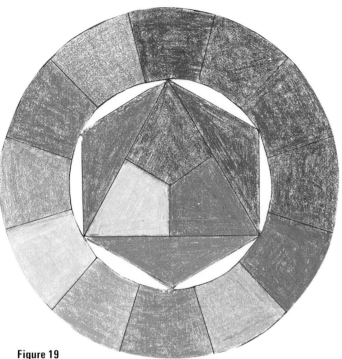

Figure 19
Colour wheel – wax crayon – exercise 10

SHADES

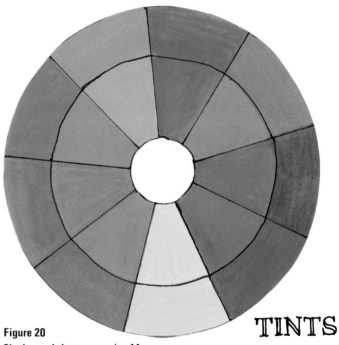

Figure 20
Shades and tints – exercise 11

TINTS

11. Secondary hues
Red + yellow = orange
Blue + red = violet
Yellow + blue = green

Working on a neutral background, use primary, secondary and tertiary colours moving in to white luminous or black shady.
Fig 20 shows how you can add black to your hue to obtain shades and white to obtain tints.

Tertiary hues
These are any mix of the three primary hues.
Note that neutral grey is a special tertiary hue.

12. Complementary hues (as in colour wheels)
Red/green
Yellow/violet
Blue/orange

These are opposite to each other on the colour wheel; discordant, in complete contrast – each pair shares no component.

Figure 21
Complementary hues – exercise 12

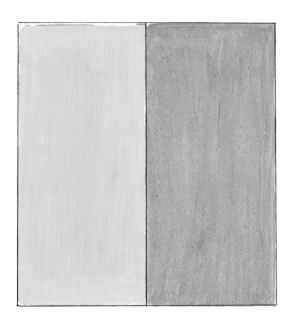

Figure 22
Analogous hues – exercise 13

13. Analogous hues
Adjacent, sharing the same components, harmonious.

Wrinkle
It is essential to do the exercises provided using clear colours (poster paints). Once these are completed the reader will find the terminology slips into place; then you can start to work out your own discords, and complementary and analogous colour schemes.

Optical fusion – sweets Author's collection

14. Optical fusion

Dots of colour mixed by the eye as did the 'Pointillist' school of painters.

Throw a few sweets onto the bench and, with felt-tip pens, paint a picture by using adjacent but separate primary hues as dots, so that if, for example, adjacent, not overlapping, yellow and blue dots are used the eye will fuse them into green. Liquorice 'Allsorts' are very useful for this exercise.

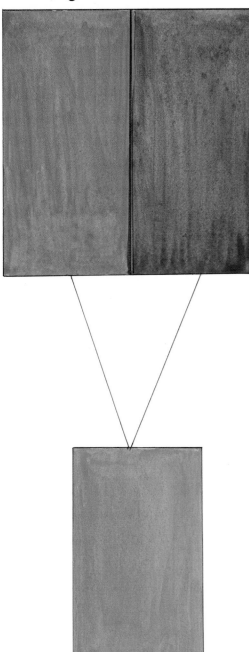

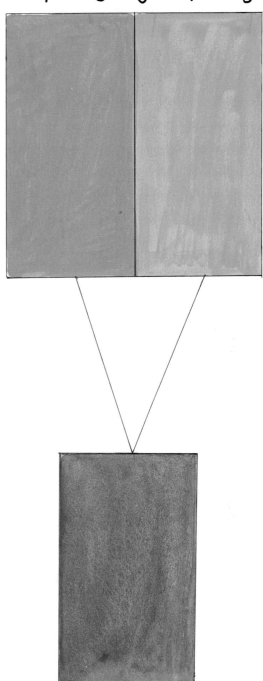

Figure 23
Split complementary hues – exercise 15

16. Discords

You should read Faber Birren, *Principles of Color*, p. 45 'Natural Law of Harmony'. Some discords are:

blue and orange, emerald green and orange, (see page 30). Now find more harmonies and discords for yourself. You will find a pro-forma drawing in the appendix to show the relationship between warm tints and cool shades to practise this point.

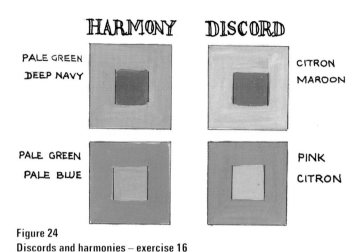

HARMONY DISCORD

PALE GREEN
DEEP NAVY

CITRON
MAROON

PALE GREEN
PALE BLUE

PINK
CITRON

Figure 24
Discords and harmonies – exercise 16

17. Colour contrasts

Using the proforma for this exercise on page 136, take six different hues and paint them on to the large squares, leaving the smaller insets blank. Then take a paler primary hue and paint that into the left hand three inset squares – leaving the border blank in square one.

Do the same with a darker primary hue for the right hand set. Notice how the primary appears to change in both hue and tonal value when superimposed on the base hues and how the white separation in the first pair of squares alters your perceptions.

18. Colour proportions

Start with a coloured postcard. List all the colours on the card, then grade each colour according to its proportions. Take a small strip of white card $1 \times 4\,\text{cm}$ ($\frac{1}{2} \times 1\frac{1}{2}\,\text{in}$) and stick a line of double-sided adhesive tape to its face. Cut out coloured paper rectangles of a suitable size and colour from, for example, magazine advertisements; then, in proportion to the amount of colours you have stated on the list, stick these to the adhesive strip on the card.

19. Ordered sequences of weight

The exercises shown opposite will help you with your choice of colours. Their modification with stitchery or the overlay of transparent fabrics and so on will give a subtle use of colour to your fabrics and thread. This may all be combined with texture to create some really exciting results.

20. Woven paper strips

When painting, wipe the surplus paint from your brush on a piece of paper; do this quite freely. When you have finished painting cut the paper into strips and weave it back into a sheet, securing it at the back with masking tape – yet another design.

Conclusion

A further study of colour is a rewarding occupation, but for the novice embroiderer the essentials can be found in this chapter.

There are several different 'schools' of colour terminology and you should study the different approaches of each theory. Refer to Faber Birren, *Principles of Color* (see Bibliography).

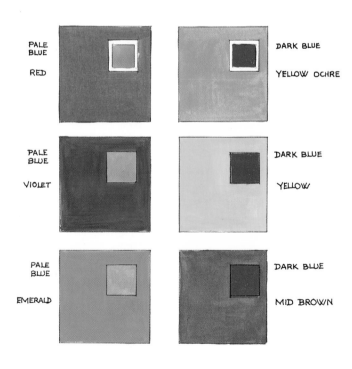

PALE
BLUE
RED

DARK BLUE
YELLOW OCHRE

PALE
BLUE
VIOLET

DARK BLUE
YELLOW

PALE
BLUE
EMERALD

DARK BLUE
MID BROWN

Figure 25
Discords and harmonies – white separation – exercise 17

ORDERED SEQUENCES OF WEIGHT

Light — W

Heavy — B

G

THIS APPEARS TO MOVE UPWARDS

B — Heavy

G

W — Light

THIS GIVES A SENSE OF PRESSURE

HAPHAZARD

B

W

G

G

B

W

Figure 26
Ordered and haphazard sequences of weight – exercise 19

REGULAR

WHITE tint
GREY tone
BLACK black

BLACK
GREY tone
WHITE tint

IRREGULAR

WHITE
BLACK
GREY

BLACK
WHITE
GREY

REVERSED

Figure 27
Regular, irregular and reversed sequences of weight – exercise 19

Woven paper strips – exercise 20

5
Methods of design

Fabric and thread exercises

Before you settle down to more formal exercises, you should make a collection of as many fabrics and threads as you can lay hands on. Cut them into 3×2 cm ($1\frac{1}{4} \times \frac{3}{4}$ in) pieces and clip them to a large piece of paper – preferably grey. Arrange them in some sort of order, giving attention to the texture of the warp and the weft and the general appearance of the weave. Familiarize yourself with the names of the fabrics and of the threads of every kind and hue. Collect ribbons, beads, string, seeds, shells, dried plants and so on. Then design yourself a mock-up embroidery.

It is always wise to make a design in scraps of fabric to assess for yourself the balance as well as the colour and texture of the design. The next three illustrations are a good introduction to balance and shape and, through the fabrics used, an introduction to texture and colour.

21. Exercise
Draw a
circle, 16 cm diameter (Fig 28, exploding the circle)
square, 16 cm × 16 cm (Fig 29, exploding the square)
rectangle, 19 cm × 16 cm (Fig 30, exploding the rectangle – straight lines)

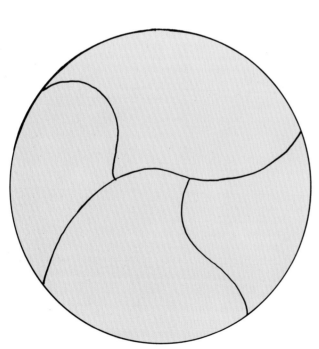

Figure 28
Exploding the circle – exercise 21

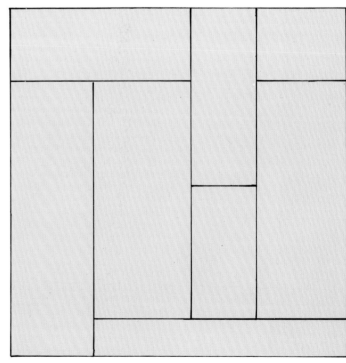

Figure 29
Exploding the square – exercise 21

rectangle, 19 cm × 16 cm (Fig 31, exploding the rectangle – curves)

triangle, sides about 13 cm long (Fig 32, exploding the triangle).

Now divide the circular, rectangular, and triangular areas as follows, referring to the illustrations:

1. The circle should be divided with curved lines into four or five areas.
2. The other three should be similarly divided with straight lines into about four or five areas of squares and rectangles.
3. The first rectangle should be divided with straight lines into five areas.
4. The second rectangle should be divided with compasses into five areas.

Work each of the five figures separately. This will help to make you aware of shapes and balance.

The triangle can be divided into three or four areas by straight lines. Cut out these figures separately and arrange them in a satisfying order on your pin-board.

Make a tracing of the shapes and use them as templates. Keep the three sets of templates separate from each other for the time being. Now cut out the templates in different fabrics. No turnings are required for this exercise, as the shapes will be stuck to sheets of paper to make a satisfying design.

Now try mixing the templates from the three basic geometric shapes into a composite design and carry this forward into fabric.

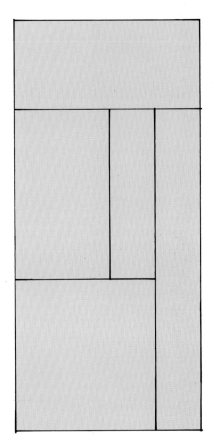

Figure 30
Exploding the rectangle –
straight lines – exercise 21

Figure 31
Exploding the rectangle –
curves – exercise 21

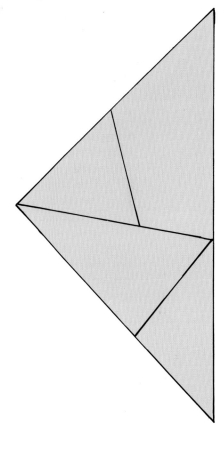

Figure 32
Exploding the triangle –
exercise 21

Figure 33
Torn paper design

22. Torn paper design

Collect coloured advertisements from the Sunday colour supplements or similar publications. Tear them into odd shapes, ignoring the original picture. Make an arrangement of these shapes without in any way consciously trying to make a picture. You will find that they will suggest something to you – for example some shape or pattern which reminds you of an engineering object, a natural thing, or a purely abstract design. Translate these shapes into fabric and enhance them with threads which will, at the same time, fasten them to the backing material. It would be helpful to place your backing material in a tambour frame to hold the work stable.

23. Fabric distortion design

Choose a 15 cm square of fabric from which threads are easily withdrawn, either from the body of the piece or to make a fringe or otherwise distort the weave; for example, loosely woven linen, tweed (preferably evenly woven), scrim or denim (which has a two-tone weave). Keep the threads you have withdrawn, because they will be used for stitching and weaving back into another fabric. By mixing roughly spun fabrics with contrasting silks, strips of cotton, cellophane, binder twine, raffia, ribbons, dried grasses and flexible sticks or board, the fabric is very effectively distorted and gives you further experience of handling materials in pursuit of a satisfying design.

Spend a 45 minute period each month on a design using paper and clipping to it the proposed fabrics and threads – 45 minutes is a sensible period to teach yourself the discipline of active work rather than day-dreaming about what might be.

Exercises of this nature are best carried out in a spirit of playfulness and good humour. The results should be kept – even when they seem to be disasters – as a cheerful record of your progress. Remember that often great mistakes contain the seeds of an idea which you have not yet recognized. Given time, your own individual style and identity as an embroiderer will be rooted in these nascent ideas.

6

Design development

You should now explore further by tearing, for example, the following kinds of material:
  tissue paper
  corrugated paper
  cardboard
  wallpaper
  laminated paper.
Do not exclude any possibilities. Go and explore! Coloured tissue paper may be torn, cut, or scrunched up and stuck to a background; it is very flexible and it is also translucent and will shape up easily into flower or plant designs.

All types of paper and card tear at different forces and leave a variety of edges which can be manipulated into a selection of shapes and objects. It is only by making your own experiments with these ideas that you will experience the possibilities and come to be able to use the medium for your own design purposes.

When making any design, do remember to keep the 'master copy' intact. Subsequent developments of the design for arrangement, colour, templates, fabrics, transfers and so on should always be made from tracings. Even when using graph paper for counted thread designs or if painting directly on the fabric, as in some canvas work, or where the painting is a part of the overall design, the original master copy must still be saved.

Other design methods

Here are some other design methods which may help those who flinch from the prospect of drawing.

Shadows and outlines
Hold a trail of ivy or some other plant between the light and your paper so that it casts a shadow; draw around the outline of the

shadow and you may have an interesting shape which you can start to develop into a design.

Develop this idea by drawing around objects placed on your paper such as a key, clothes peg, a piece of bone, a paper clip, a pair of scissors, cutlery, a spanner or some other tool or artefact. By repeating these shapes in a formal or informal layout you may produce another basis for the long process of design refinement.

Focusing designs
Designs need to be focused. One way to help do this is to make a 'viewfinder' or 'window' to concentrate the eye. Make two 'L' shapes 25 cm × 10 cm and 4 cm in cross section out of firm cardboard. Form them into a square and

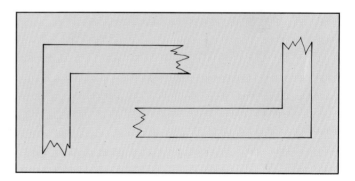

Figure 34
'Viewfinder'

move them about the illustration, contracting and expanding the shape in both directions until they frame a satisfactory design. Fix them in position and make a tracing. When sketching out of doors, use a cardboard rectangle to frame the area of hedge, bush or whatever you wish to sketch.

Projecting designs
Take two pieces of transparent acetate film and place between them anything you like,

such as a dead fly, a squiggle of wool, a few sequins, moss, and similar things. Place this sandwich into an old photographic slide holder and use a slide projector to project it on a firm surface. Place a piece of tracing paper over the image and trace off the abstract design.

Contact printing

On a sheet of glass place a paper frame 15 cm × 10 cm (cut two). Pick a random handful of grasses and weeds from a bank, spread it carelessly over the paper frame and fix the second paper frame over the first, trapping the handful of plants. Using a roller, apply a thick lino-cut paint or a similar medium. Reverse the 'sandwich' on a sheet of paper and roll off several copies.

These are only a few methods of starting to develop a design for those who find drawing a problem. This does not replace designing with pencil and brush from scratch, but is meant as a way to let the reader in gently. Do not neglect to study the numerous books on design for embroidery and learn how earlier generations of embroiderers have learnt to build on a tradition and develop it into something quite new.

Doodling

It is good practice to draw or even to 'doodle' for not less than 20 minutes a day because it increases your facility to sketch your ideas swiftly as well as increasing your powers of observation, which is what design is about. Now you will begin to realize the value of those sketch books which I hope you will by now have filled with many observations. Your camera is a further medium of design, reducing a three-dimensional view to the flat surface of the print.

Figure 35
Plant sandwich print

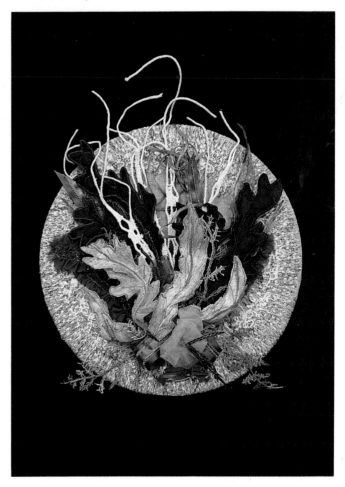

◀ **Seaweed research** Jeanette Morton

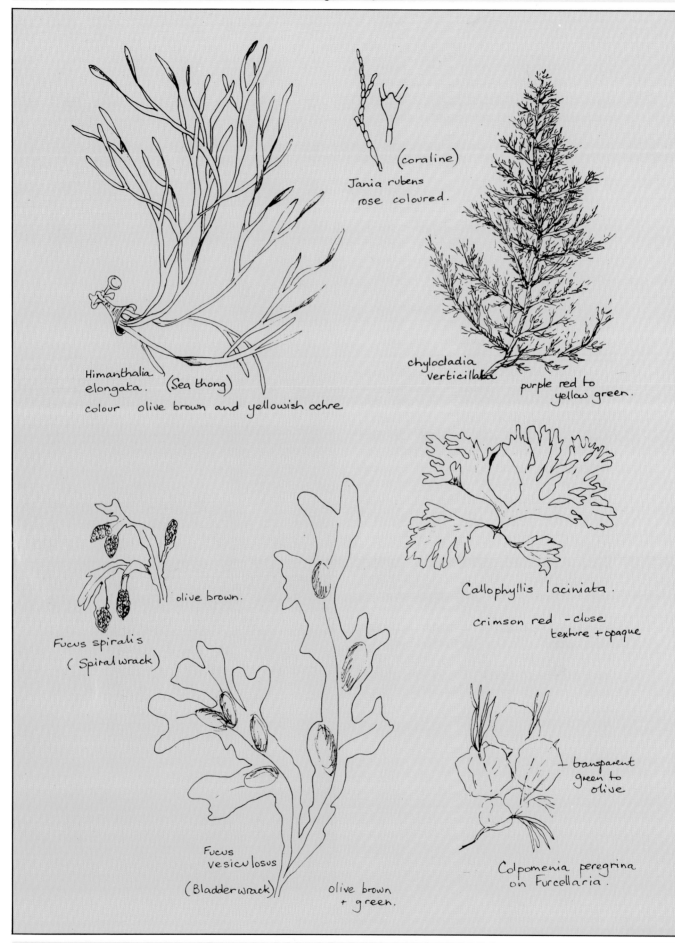

(coraline)
Jania rubens
rose coloured.

Himanthalia
elongata. (Sea thong)
colour olive brown and yellowish ochre.

chylocladia
Verticillata   purple red to
                     yellow green.

olive brown.

Fucus spiralis
(Spiral wrack)

Callophyllis laciniata.

crimson red – close
         texture + opaque

Fucus
vesiculosus

(Bladderwrack)   olive brown
                  + green.

transparent
green to
olive

Colpomenia peregrina
on Furcellaria.

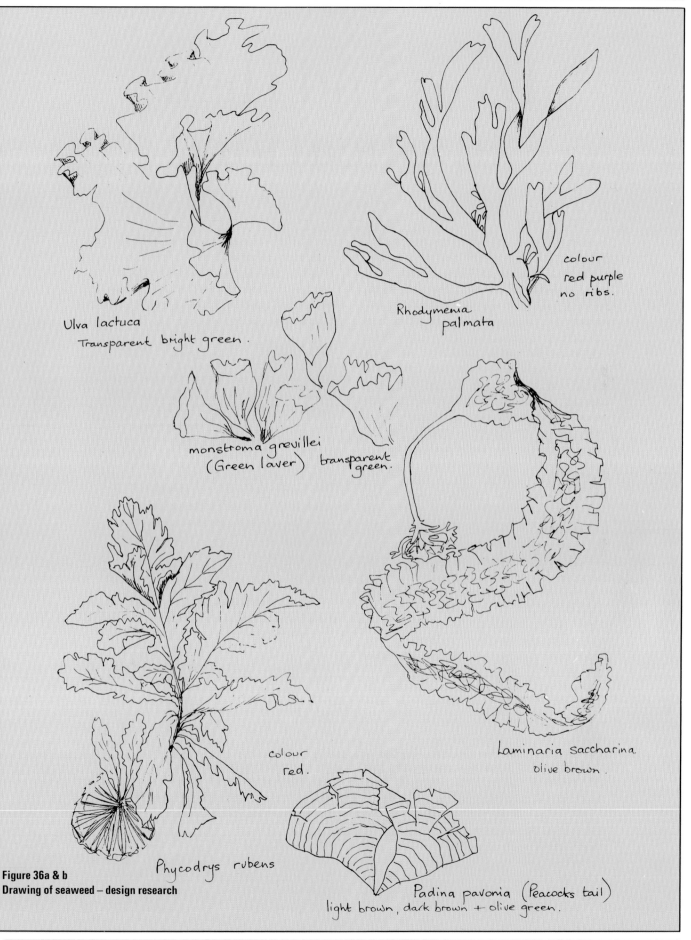

Ulva lactuca
Transparent bright green.

Rhodymenia
palmata

colour
red purple
no ribs.

monstroma grevillei
(Green laver) transparent
green.

colour
red.

Laminaria saccharina
olive brown.

Phycodrys rubens

Padina pavonia (Peacocks tail)
light brown, dark brown + olive green.

Figure 36a & b
Drawing of seaweed – design research

7
Dyes and their application

In recent decades embroidery has rejoined the fine arts. The days of working a few cross-stitches on a pre-printed design from a kit using stranded cotton, or of completing embroidery packs are, mercifully, over. No self-respecting embroiderer will work a commercially designed piece; instead the embroiderer will make the design for his or her own embroidery and choose the best fabric and thread, and this is where dyeing and fabric painting can add to your experience. There are many dyes to choose from, as well as ways of making them fast and of choosing the hue and tone required for a particular piece of work.

Dye types

When you choose your dye be careful that it is appropriate to the fabric yarns, and learn how to use it properly. Be aware of the chemistry of dyes and read the instructions with care to avoid accidents both to yourself and to your fabric.

Remember that some dyes will not work on some fabrics. For example, dyes for cellulose fabrics, such as cotton, will not necessarily work using the same technique on protein-based fibres, such as wool. Protein-based fibres may require hot-dye processes.

Remember, too, that some dyes can be destructive to some fibres unless used carefully. For example, salt can rot silk after prolonged contact, so consult the instructions. Always use a fabric that has been thoroughly washed to get rid of any dressing material that is on the fibres. Similarly, rinse the dyed fabric thoroughly to rid it of excess dye chemicals.

Dyes come in various families and are distinguished by whether they react with the fibre itself or with a second chemical with which the fabric has been pre-treated, and by how the dye reaction is set fast. You should familiarize yourself with the qualities and disadvantages of acid, basic, direct, mordant, reactive, and vat dyes. You may enjoy experimenting wih the Azoic dyestuffs which are sometimes available in domestic quantities from dye suppliers.

Safety first

Use overalls, gloves and eye protection. Do not spill dyes on your skin or into your eyes; avoid breathing in dye powders — even in small quantities, these are not necessarily as harmless to you as the advertising may suggest. Avoid dyeing in hot vats when there are small children and animals around, and don't use your ordinary kitchen pots and pans — aluminium and hot soda love each other to their mutual destruction. Enamel or stainless steel is reliable for hot vats, polythene for cold. Wooden spoons can absorb dye chemicals and could give your family Doctor some curious puzzles in the future, so be aware and use your common sense.

Bleach is dangerous and will rot fabric, so use it diluted and sparingly with sensible precautions such as overalls, gloves, and eye protection. Always rinse the material thoroughly and immediately after the required effect has been obtained.

Bleach

Bleach is a useful way of making a 'negative' and works well on a fabric that is not dye-fast – for example cotton denim – tied and dipped, splattered or masked. There are also other products which will remove some dyes in part or whole which do less damage.

Special silk dyes

Special dyes that are particularly good for silk fabrics are available. These retain the sheen of the silk and are also useful for threads that have a sheen of their own, for example mercerized cotton and perlé.

Iron-on dyes

With cotton and polycotton fabrics, the design may be painted on the fabric and ironed to make it fast. If the design has been made with a conscious intent to fill out the dye with stitchery, quilting, beading, and so on, then you will need to plan how you will arrange your dye and what technique and stitchery you will be using beforehand. There are excellent instructions for use printed on the dye packaging.

Paint your design (reversed) on paper and then iron on to the fabric. Polycotton is an ideal fabric for this method. One painting can be ironed several times; each press diminishes the amount of dye deposited, which offers a wonderful opportunity for experimentation.

Tie-dyeing

This is always fun as there are so many possibilities, depending on how the fabric is tied. Some suggestions: tie jagged stones firmly into some pre-washed calico, taking careful note of each stone's shape and the manner of tying, because it is possible to create the particular shapes you require, such as a flower, bird or animal. Each tied stone could be dipped in a different hue or tone of one hue. Thin fabric may be gathered together in a length and knotted or tied at intervals. Fabric may also be firmly pleated and held together with stitching or clothes pegs – both will add another texture to the pattern. Batik uses a resist wax to create an outline, and also makes it possible to dip a fabric into a succession of colours. You must plan your colour scheme ahead to build up your design.

Home-made dyes

Home-made vegetable dyes have particularly muted tones and are not always light and wash-fast. They require a great deal of know-ledge and skill to obtain true, bright, clear colours. An amoebic sludge colour is all too easy to create in dyeing!

Methods of applying dyes

Block printing

Use a fabric printing dye. Blocks are best made with balsa wood as it is easy to obtain and to carve. Make a block with a simple repetitive design, dip it into the dye and block this on your fabric. Remember that the fabric must be held firm and undistorted before attempting to block print. Screws of corrugated paper, halved potatoes and cotton reel ends are all useful.

Impression printing

Use some thick dye or fabric paint, and spread it on a flat glass surface; place a leaf or whatever unevenly-surfaced shape you have made on the paint and roll it firmly, then lift it and place it on your fabric in the appropriate place and roll it again firmly; you can do this several times with one load of colour, and each impression will be a little paler.

Spray dyeing

Cut a simple pattern or stencil and place it firmly on the fabric; then spray, obtaining a different texture by the pressure of the spray and the speed at which your hand traverses the fabric. Where the spray lingers, it is denser and the tone deepens. Where the spray moves fast, the effect is more open.

Masking

Leaves, shapes, outlines of birds and animals or other easily recognized objects or abstract shapes will give exciting opportunities for designs. The shapes acting as masks are revealed after spraying and lend themselves to a variety of stitchery and quilting. The masked-out area can, of course, be sprayed in turn.

Random printing or splattering

Use a piece of frayed string dipped in your dye and flick it on the fabric – and not elsewhere!

Stencil printing

Fold a piece of firm paper in four and then cut small shapes from it; open the paper out and stipple with a brush through the pattern. These designs are useful for quilting.

Pastel dye crayons

Use these to draw a colouring on the fabric; moisten them and the colours will suffuse in a more or less delicate fashion – very useful for backgrounds.

Comments

All these methods of using dyes will be experiments for you, as it is not usually possible at low levels of skill to predict exactly how your efforts will turn out. Do not be inhibited – seize the opportunity to enjoy and learn from the surprises. Your mistakes, especially, will be turned to good use, so always record exactly how you worked.

Net, or some diaphonous fabric, can be placed over your dyed fabric to add interest and tone; this method creates 'shadows'.

8
Basic stitches

I suggest that you approach stitches in the following manner: make some samplers for yourself, practising the stitches mentioned below in a simple but pleasing design of your own, not being afraid to vary them in size, direction and choice of thread. Stitches may be used one over another in depth. Do plenty of this type of stitchery and be inventive. The simplest stitch will often prove the most effective if used sympathetically in conjunction with another.

A swing needle sewing machine offers further possibilities, and of course with the machine it is possible to create new effects; it can also offer a quick way of working in a background. Machine embroidery as such will be dealt with in Chapter 15.

Meanwhile, consult the books on stitchery that are listed in the Bibliography. This is not the place to give diagrams of stitches: that has been covered amply in other textbooks. My aim is to open up the possibilities that lie before you and to encourage you to experiment and to achieve your own original and independent use of stitchery.

Stitch families

Stitches may be divided roughly into five families, as follows:

straight
looped
knotted
crossed
laid and couched.

In addition, there is a very wide variety of composite stitches.

The following five exercises are designed to introduce you to the great variety of embroidery stitches and the part they will play in the design and practice of your embroideries, if you can make them work for you.

Straight stitches

These are the least complicated stitches, but you can devise many patterns by running, darning, backstitching or simply by using a straight stitch in random fashion. Often quite large stitches can give the impression of 'hatching', a form of dense line drawing making a dark shadow or light indicating a shape. You will have met this procedure in the floor exercise (see Chapter 3) when areas were filled with lines formed with a ruler placed in various directions. Now make your own sampler, referring to several of the books on this subject listed in the Bibliography.

Looped stitches

Looped stitches are formed when the needle passes through the loop made by the previous stitch, as in the various forms of chain and buttonhole stitches. When the loops begin to open out they form a herringbone group of stitches.

These straight and looped stitches may be worked over by others, and they then become composite stitches, as in looped running stitch and whipped stem stitch. A similar treatment is possible with the chain stitches – raised chain band is a good example.

Now work another sampler. In this way you will gather together in your loose-leaf folder a variety of useful samples to refer to when choosing stitches.

Knotted stitches

The round shape of the french knot and the long shape of the bullion knot are the foundation of knotted stitches; but there are many varieties and uses of these. For example, coral stitch is a variant of the French knot strung together with the surface stitch. Bullion stitch may be worked over a cord laid upon the surface and resembles a rope. There are many such composite stitches for you to copy or invent for yourself. Keep them as practical sampler demonstrations to refer to later.

Crossed stitches
These are very familiar stitches which occur in the embroidery of almost every country and are worked over counted threads. They are used in many ways, on canvas, linen, as a background filling as in 'voiding' as the filling of a shape whether natural or abstract, and in repetitive design. You can experiment for

yourself using a variety of suitable counted-thread fabrics and varied threads.

Laid and couched stitches
These are grouped together because they are so alike. These stitches are truly 'surface' stitches: the thread lies on the surface of the fabric and is couched down.

Laid work is always couched and couched work is used to secure a thread on the surface. Laid work is where a thread is laid across the surface of the fabric from side to side of the area in the design which is to be covered. The stitch does not pass along under the back as in satin

Crossed stitches Lorna Rand

Jellyfish – pencil Lorna Rand

Jellyfish – colour. Couching page 47

stitch, but instead picks up a very small thread of the fabric and returns, repeating the exercise until the whole area is covered.

These long laid stitches must be couched down to hold them in place, using a single thread laid at right angles. This long thread is couched in turn by a small stitch which passes through the fabric at regular intervals. Stem stitch and fly stitch are sometimes used for this purpose. For example, the stem stitch could describe the veins of a leaf embroidered in laid work and a fly stitch could represent the speckled surface of a strawberry. Look closely at old embroideries and you will see how the stitches are used to suggest the surface or texture of the shape that the design depicts. Books on gold work and metal threads have good examples of laid and couched work.

Couched stitch is for laying a thread, as when laying gold thread (which never passes through the fabric) and indeed any other

thread you wish to keep on the surface. Sometimes the stitching of appliqué is hidden by couching round the edge.

Ruching is another specialized kind of couched surface stitch often used when transferring old embroideries to new fabric backgrounds. Place a suitable thread over the embroidery edge and then couch it down firmly, slightly easing the thread as you couch.

Long stitches will inevitably be either too tight, puckering the fabric, or too loose, hanging slack. To find the proper tension it is necessary to use a frame. You will quickly notice that the tension of the fabric in the frame has a strong effect on the results when you remove the finished piece. If the fabric has been over-stretched in the frame, then all the stitches will hang loose, and vice-versa.

Samplers
It is essential to make your own samplers – and in the order set out in this book; they will be invaluable to you and it is a good way to come to know your stitches.

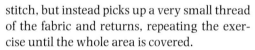

◀ **Christmas baubles, laid and couched**

9

Traditional stitches

Assisi Lorna Rand

Assisi

History

This is a variety of Italian cross stitch which shows the pattern by 'voiding'. It originated in Assisi in the fifteenth century. Study the Renaissance period Spanish work, and also that of the Moors, for design. Italian and Spanish designs are chiefly geometric or heraldic. The 'voiding' may have come from Egypt (Egyptian inlay designs in pearl and ivory). The association with cross stitch is comparatively recent: antique pieces use backstitch, buttonhole and whipped running stitches. 'Punto Scritto' is the name given to the outline stitch. Long-arm cross was also used in the background.

Method

The design is 'voided', that is, drawn like a photographic negative, and outlined in double running stitch with the background filled in with cross stitch.

Materials

Linen fabric, single threads. Traditional colours are red and blue, but a single 'pure' colour also works.

Sampler

Try an heraldic animal – the effect is very plain and dignified.

Wrinkles

When turning a corner with any repetitive design, use a small mirror placed at an angle of 45 degrees to the corner; this helps to keep the design flowing.

Blackwork

History

This Mediterranean technique, also known as Holbein work or Spanish work, may have come from North Africa with the settlement in Spain from AD 700 onwards by the Moors. It concentrates on plants and intricate patterns because of the Islamic taboo on the representation of the human form. There is evidence that it was known in Europe before Catherine of Aragon, who is reputed to have brought the technique, came to England.

Method

The technique is to use threads of varying thicknesses with a variety of counted thread stitches. By choosing a dense stitch for dark areas and an open stitch for the light areas a pattern can be built up to accommodate your design. Objects are represented by exploring tones in just one contrasting hue, usually black. Today red or navy blue is sometimes used, and occasionally metallic thread in very small quantities. The work is traditionally soft and the worked stitching should neither distort nor stiffen the base fabric. Three basic stitches are used: back stitch, cross stitch and double running stitch. Many other stitches may be used as fillings.

Materials

Fine linen, black thread, sometimes a little metal thread; for example, gold passing thread is used to add a flourish.

Sampler

Used on collars, sleeves and underwear. See Tudor and Stuart portraits.

Wrinkles

Use evenweave fabric and, according to the effect required, any thread from a 60 cotton to buttonhole thread. Avoid enlarging the fabric mesh with too large a needle. Avoid creating unsought perspective by overdoing the tonal differences between pattern and background.

Blackwork Lorna Rand

Canvas Work

History

Before the invention of open-weave canvas, which became available in the last century, people tried to emulate wall-hanging woven tapestries by using tent stitch on an even-weave, rough, unbleached linen. This was sometimes called 'Poor Man's Tapestry'. When open evenweave canvas became available with Berlin work, the same technique was applied and was loosely referred to as 'tapestry work', hence the confusion between tapestry (which is woven on a loom) and canvas embroidery, called needlepoint in the USA.

Method

There are so many stitches suitable for canvas work that it would be better to consult the Bibliography for books from which to choose your stitches. There are some 300 suitable

Water wheel – canvas work Sereta Thompson

stitches, and, according to the mesh of your fabric and the thickness of your thread, you can make your own choice. Note that there are two kinds of canvas to work on, single or double. Sometimes it is useful to use the double canvas because you can 'prick' the double threads apart and work them as a single mesh using a finer thread. This adds texture and interest to your design.

Materials

The canvas used today is usually made specifically for canvas embroidery, but a coarse, evenweave fabric is acceptable. Raffia, strips of fine cotton fabric, ribbons, wool, string and plastic are all grist to your mill when making an exciting design for your canvas stitches.

Sampler

Work small blocks of a varied selection of stitches on a variety of fabrics. When these are mounted, leave a small margin of the background fabric visible to show the affinity of stitch, thread and fabric.

Wrinkles

The canvas must be mounted on a frame before starting to stitch. This needs to be a square frame, not circular – except for very fine fabric. The raw edges should be bound with masking tape to avoid the annoyance of threads catching on the canvas edge.

Pear – counted thread work Ella Pratt

Jacobean work

History

Work of the Tudor period was succeeded by Jacobean embroidery, which is characterized by a more elaborate use of stitchery, especially crewel work, to cover the fabric entirely with traceries of plant forms. The old name for this, 'crewel', meant 'wool embroidery work' in the sixteenth century when it was popular. The embellishment of the home, which was by then becoming more comfortable, required cushions, bed hangings, table-carpets, book-bindings and even decorative sword scabbards for the elaborate costumes of the courtiers. Look for examples of these in the Victoria and Albert Museum and several English country houses, notably Hardwick Hall in Derbyshire, where Bess of Hardwick was an enthusiastic embroideress, as was also Mary, Queen of Scots, some of whose work is also to be found there.

The technique was revived in the twentieth century as an alternative to the nineteenth-century Berlin wool work, so called because the first dyes were produced from coal tar in the country now known as Germany, and the King of Prussia had introduced the very fine, soft-fleeced Merino breed of sheep to Prussia, of which Berlin was the capital. Here, too, the first embroidery canvas was produced. The wool, canvas and dyes were brought together and used as a form of upholstery. The designs were originally taken from woven tapestries, hence the confusion between the modern term 'tapestry work' and the true term 'canvas work' given to the first 'kits' – which then went out of fashion due to over-exposure!

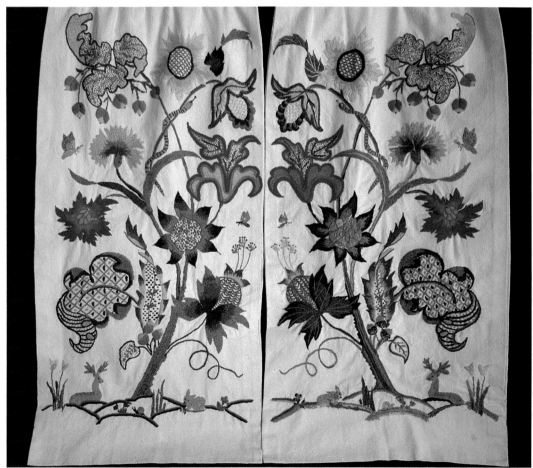

Curtains Gladys Dennett and Grace Parker

Method

Chunky outline stitches and a variety of filling stitches.

Materials

Twill (a mixture of thick cotton and wool) with a chevron weave, and 'crewel' wools.

Sampler

Look at some of the old samplers illustrated in books and you will find 'The Tree of Life' growing out of 'Terra Firma' and several heraldic animals. Needlewomen of the time used 'slips' (i.e. illustrations of plant cuttings from seventeenth-century books about gardening) for their designs.

Wrinkles

Beware the popular designs for these dating from the 1920s and 1930s. The reduction of the large sixteenth-century designs for use on smaller articles, as you will know from your exercises in design, is not always successful.

Florentine (also known as Bargello)

History

This is Italian work on canvas or evenweave fabrics, used chiefly in upholstery. Some very early examples show traditional designs such as flame, carnation, and Hungarian point. The design is by counted thread and has a distinctive 'up and down' effect as it is worked in a strictly methodical manner. Usually the threads (wool or mercerized cotton) are of three or four tones of one hue and a contrast hue to define the repetition of the design.

Method

Use a dark colour to divide and give accent to the design which is usually worked in analogous hues and tones of a single hue, geometric shapes and repetitive patterns.

Materials

Wool on single canvas.

Sampler

Try many combinations of colour, making

Prie-Dieu Author's collection

your own design which can have a pointed or a distinctly rounded pattern. The 'onion' shaped domes of Russian Orthodox churches would make an excellent sampler. You can vary your work with any thread provided it has relevance to the design and use of the article.

Wrinkles

A frame is a necessity and there is ample opportunity for brilliant colour combinations. Single canvas should be used and the thread must cover the canvas if you want the work to wear well.

Smocking

History
An ancient, probably Saxon, method of gathering a fabric into a flexible shape. The smock, which is of peasant origin, is probably the most familiar garment to use this technique, but it has become widely used, particularly on children's garments, where a certain elasticity plus fullness are a necessity.

Method
A fine, regular check, lined or spotted fabric should be used. If a plain or patterned fabric is to be used, the regular dots must be made on the reverse side and these must be in an evenly spaced straight line about 1 cm in each direction.

The fabric should be about three times the width of the finished article. Using a strong thread, pick up each dot and when the whole area to be covered is completed draw the threads up two at a time and secure them with a pin. Turn to the right side of your fabric and note the 'tubes' – these must be even. It is possible to use a shirring or pleating machine for this, but most embroiderers are happy with hand-gathered threads. Use DMC mercerized cotton, 'Filoselle' silk, or a similar coloured thread to suit the fabric. A linen self-match thread looks well on natural linen, particularly if the smock is like the traditional working garment which may have the decorative designs. It used to be said that these designs denoted the wearer's occupation and county, but this is no longer thought to be so.

There are a number of stitches to choose from, for example chain, cable, rope, basket, honeycomb, to name but a few, and it is the individual's choice to arrange them for a satisfying design.

Materials
Fabric: crêpe de chine, 'Viyella', cotton, calico, holland. Threads in silk, cotton and linen are all suitable.

Smocking Lorna Rand

Sampler
A child's smock.

Wrinkles
Don't try to skimp on the fullness of the garment.

10

Whitework stitches

How this chapter works

Whitework is a generic name for the domestic embroidery of household linen and underclothes. Each area of Europe has a distinct tradition, but these are now widely known and embroidery has borrowed from and integrated these techniques.

This chapter reflects this, and is a survey of the main traditions familiar in English embroidery; the links between them will offer the student a first-class research opportunity and you will find plenty of references in the Bibliography to help you on your way.

Ayrshire – Scotland

Open needlepoint filling on fine muslin. Uses pulled work, satin and beading stitches in very fine thread. Popular in the early nineteenth century.

Broderie Anglaise – England

Eyelet embroidery: a type of cut work, which evolved in Britain in about 1850 from the earlier Ayrshire embroidery and quickly became very popular. When exported to Madeira it became known as Madeira work. You may also study the books by Etta Campbell and Elsie Svennas on lettering (see Bibliography).

Water lily Ella Pratt

Filet lace Lorna Rand

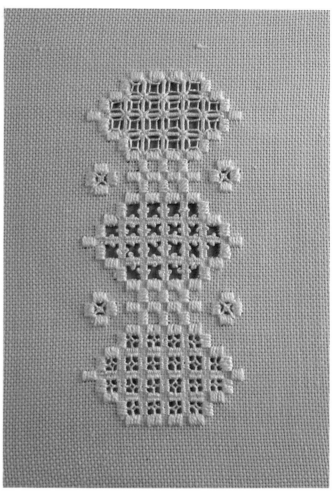

Hedebo Lorna Rand

Cut work

This includes those techniques known as Reticella, Richelieu, and Ruskin work (or Greek lace) – see pages 59 and 60.

Filet lace (filet darning, or lacis)

First make your own net with square 5 mm ($\frac{1}{4}$ in) mesh on a 15 cm (6 in) or 20 cm ($7\frac{3}{4}$ in) metal frame. The geometric pattern is formed by darning squares to make the pattern.

Hardanger – Norway

From that district of Norway. Blocks of geometric satin stitch alternate with squares of cut threads. These blocks are called 'klosters'. The characteristic ground fabric is an even-weave linen.

Hedebo – Denmark

This originated near Copenhagen, matured from the middle seventeenth century from a cut and drawn threadwork style with surface embroidery, adding various fillings during the early nineteenth century from Italian cut work, and then losing its drawn thread work in favour of complex lace stitches as the work became better known elsewhere.

Hemstitch

Embroidery of hems: drawn threads are replaced by making small bundles of thread into decorative features. The more threads drawn, the greater the opportunity to make decorative patterns. Examples of this work may be found on table linen of the nineteenth century, usually worked in India for the English market.

Mountmellick – Ireland

A set group of stitches which appear to have been taken from Jacobean embroidery and developed by Quakers at Mountmellick, near Waterford in Ireland, during the 1840s famine. The work has a rather heavy, coarse and unsophisticated look. Designs were developed from hedgerow plants. The edge was normally buttonholed, but there is also a knitted type of fringe peculiar to this tradition. Used for bedspreads, cushion covers, washstand covers and mats.

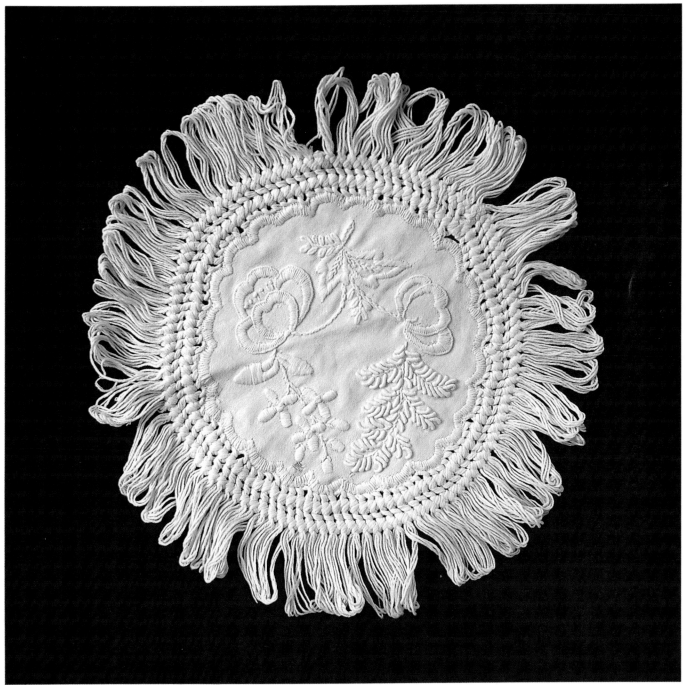

Mountmellick Author's collection

Needlelace Lorna Rand

Needleweaving

Threads are woven or darned to replace withdrawn threads. Common in Sweden and the Slavonic countries, this technique is also worked in colours. It is varied and interesting; study it further and refer to Gay Swift, *The Batsford Encyclopaedia of Embroidery Techniques*.

Net embroidery

In 1809 John Heathcote introduced a machine that produced a hexagonal net called 'Bobbinet'. The lace makers' monopoly was broken and needle-run lace on net was produced for the first time. Since then it has become a 'lace' in its own right, imitating to some extent Limerick and Carrickmacross lace.

Method

Prepare your design and transfer it to a firm and polished material such as buckram or thick paper. Place the net over the design and, using masking tape to hold it in position, tack the two together.

First outline the design by threading through the net with a running stitch in and out of each hole as if darning. This method is used throughout for a geometric design. For a realistic design, there will be a variety of areas, as in the petals of a flower, and for these you should choose a variety of filling stitches. There are many to choose from – e.g. eyelets, herringbone, or satin stitches, which give ridges and lattice effects.

Materials

Net embroidery is worked on good quality hexagonal net or on fine *toile*. The thread for the outlines should pass through the net smoothly using a blunt ended needle.

Sampler

A repeat pattern for a lace collar.

Wrinkles

Work in a frame. Strong nylon curtain with a hexagonal mesh should be used.

Pulled Work – Denmark

Also known as drawn fabric work. In the past, pulled work was worked on a fine evenweave linen or cambric. Ayrshire work is an offshoot and always done on fine cambric. Today, embroiderers use a thick needle and fine thread on evenweave linen.

The distortion of the fabric by the use of a particular stitch determines the pattern. No fabric is cut away, neither are any threads withdrawn.

In the eighteenth century in Germany this technique flourished under the name Dresden work, and is now widespread in Scandinavia.

Reticella

This is an Italian cut work bordering on lace, popular from the fifteenth to the seventeenth century in Venice. The threads are cut away and the edges buttonholed to make square geometric patterns. Threads are added to make criss-cross patterns which are also buttonhole-stitched.

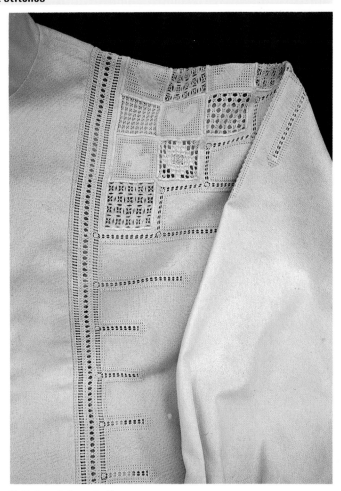

Pulled work Jeanette Morton

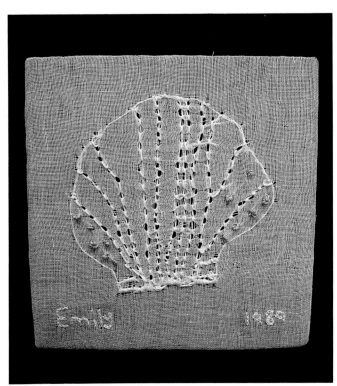

Pulled work Emily Pratt – aged four years

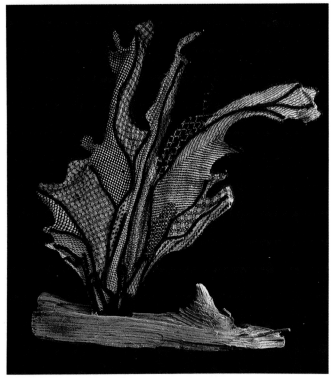

Pulled work Elizabeth Jacoby

Richelieu

Richelieu is a form of cut work named after Cardinal Richelieu of France. The design is outlined in buttonhole stitch and, before it is cut away, the several parts of the design are held in place with 'brides'. These are bars of buttonhole stitch which sometimes have a picot knot at their centre.

Ruskin work

This uses the same technique as Reticella, and is a square design on evenweave linen. Brought to Westmorland in the 1880s by Albert Fleming's housekeeper, it was backed by John Ruskin through his Guilds. It is a form of Greek lace which was very common in the fifteenth century in Greece and was called Reticella in Italy.

simple

renaissance

richlieu

italian

Cut work Lorna Rand

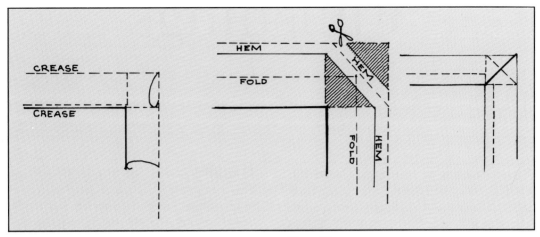

Figure 37
To mitre a corner

To mitre a corner

When finishing a piece of whitework you will
need to make neat hems. Fig 37 shows how to
mitre a corner.

A guide to materials used in traditional whitework embroideries

Embroidery	Country	Base fabric	Thread type
Ayrshire	Scotland	cambric, Swiss muslin	100's cotton
Broderie Anglaise	England	cambric	DMC mercerised cotton
Cut work:			
Reticella	Italy	close-woven linen or cotton	DMC mercerised cotton
Richelieu	France	evenweave linen	linen
Ruskin Work	UK-Lake District	evenweave linen	linen
Hardanger	Norway	evenweave linen	matching mercerised cotton
Hedebo	Sweden	as Hardanger	as Hardanger
Hemstitch	all Europe	handkerchief linen	fine cotton
Mountmellick	Ireland	coarse linen/cotton twill	DMC mercerised cotton
Needleweaving	all Europe	evenweave fabric, huckaback	DMC cotton perlé
Pulled work	Holland	lawn, evenweave, scrim	fine cotton
Smocking	UK	fabric for gathering	silk, cotton, linen

Note about materials

These are sometimes approximations to the
original materials. To obtain all of the traditional fabrics and threads would be difficult,
so a certain licence may be appropriate at this
stage in your experience. Knowing the traditional fabrics and threads helps you to
appreciate the work of the past and will enable
you to recognize work and to place it in its
historical perspective.

Samplers

Try to sort these out and work small samplers
using a variety of linens and cottons appropriate to the technique.

11
Finishings

To complete any piece of work it will sometimes be necessary to make a finishing. There is a wide range of traditional options and solutions, some of which are drawn to your attention below. It would be a pity to buy ready-made ones when, as we know from articles made before the advent of manufactured fastenings, these can all made by hand and are a delight to work in their own right.

Fringes

Any material that unravels easily can be frayed and knotted in groups to form an interesting fringe, as is found on some heavily embroidered silk shawls.

Tassels

Many shapes of tassels exist: some are constructed first over a piece of card, the loops being tied tightly together at one end while the other end is cut through. Using the tie from the top end, thread it through a wooden bead, pull tight, and knot. The loops will then cover the bead and will need to be tied firmly around the other end of it. You can embroider over these loops in detached buttonhole stitch, giving the head of the tassel a finished appearance.

Toggles

These can be made from spare fabric from the article itself. A narrow strip of the material is rolled up tightly, turning in the last fold and stitching invisibly. The ends of this roll can then be gently frayed or, alternatively, the strip of material can be turned in upon itself before it is rolled up. Suitable decorative stitching may be used.

Frogging

This is not only a decorative couched cord or braid which you make yourself, but it also serves to loop over the toggle to fasten two edges together. This embroidery is often found on waistcoats of national dress and dress uniforms.

Braids and cords

A great many decorative cords can be made, all of which are suited to couching. Braids are sometimes flat plaits and sometimes needle-woven across several strands of yarn 'warp'.

Turkish knots

These form a very useful raised button. They are easier to make with a fairly thick cord. Take a 15 cm length of cord. Make three loops between your thumb and forefinger, and pass the loose starting end through each loop. Pull the three threaded loops together very gently and – there is the button.

Buttons

The classical English button is the Dorset button. These are made over a bone or rustless wire ring. Bind the ring with buttonhole stitch and 'slick' it by turning the purl (the knobbly bit) of the stitch into the centre of the button ring. Make the spokes of the wheel by criss-crossing the thread, picking up from either side, and then needleweave from the centre outwards, making the pattern as you go. There are many other named traditional patterns for you to research.

Faggoting

Also known as 'insertion' and 'openwork seams'. This work was used to join two materials together in a decorative way to take the place of a seam. These seams can be very richly worked and may include needleweaving and braiding.

Handmade fastenings might be considered redundant; however, all these techniques have lingered to give embroidery a professional touch with fastenings that are in themselves an enhancement of your work.

You will find a good selection of finishings in Thérèse de Dillmont's *Encyclopaedia of Needle-work*, in Mary Thomas' *Embroidery Book* and in Mrs Archibald Christie's *Samplers and Stitches*.

To avoid crushing your finishings when you are mounting them in a folder, make a shallow frame from the lip of a box lid following the instructions in Jane Lemon's book, *Embroidered Boxes*. Attach this frame to an A4 sheet ready for insertion into your sampler folder.

12
Patchwork

Patchwork uses appliqué as part of its repertoire of design, and is often quilted. Hence the confusion that has arisen on this subject: 'quilting' and 'patchwork' are each techniques in their own right and will be discussed under their own headings.

History

Patchwork – known in the past as 'piece work' – is a very ancient craft and some of the oldest pieces have been found in the excavation of ancient tombs – see the examples of Persian work in the Victoria and Albert Museum. It has always been an economical domestic approach to the use of fabric for making clothes and warm coverings, and has its own folk traditions.

Some of the earliest known patchwork came from the Silk Road in China. It dated from approximately the tenth century BC, was found in the Buddha Caves at Dunghuan and was made of leather and skins now 3,000 years old. In the eighteenth century there was a blossoming of patchwork using printed calico. Today there are so many fabrics to choose from, and so many variations as well, that you will have to spend quite some time in researching the following pointers.

Traditionally English patchwork is made from cut-out, interlocking shapes based on the triangle from which hexagons, squares and diamonds are formed. Enlarge these figures by adding further triangles and other shapes emerge.

The choice of shape used dictates the design, while the use of the scraps of discarded fabric dictates the colour and overall appearance of the article. These can be quite elaborate and need a familiarity with geometric shapes to achieve the traditional symmetric approach to the pattern.

The Society of Friends, also known as the Quakers, has been responsible for much dissemination of patchwork. They would visit emigré ships and give the passengers pieces of fabric, thread, scissors and needles to make 'quilts' during the long and difficult voyages. The articles emigrés made demonstrated their ability and could be sold on arrival at their destination.

English patchwork

Templates

English patchwork is made with templates. A master shape is cut from a stiff material, then a secondary shape, 5 mm larger, is made, and it is from this that the fabric is cut. The fabric is folded over the paper shape and tacked accurately, taking care to keep the corners sharp. The most useful templates are the window type, which give the outer shape for the fabric and the inner shape for the card in one template. The inner shape, being cut away, also acts as a window, which is very useful for design purposes.

Method

The fabric must be cut on the grain – aligned to the warp and weft. It should be folded neatly over the paper and then each corner tacked carefully so that the shape is maintained exactly. These shapes are then sewn together. Place the patches back to back, with the fabric touching, and the paper on the outside and visible. Lay the 'straight of the goods' edge to edge together; i.e. avoid the edge which is cut on the cross being aligned with a straight edge and so causing a bulge or ruckle in the finished article. The two edges are then oversewn together with ten stitches to the centimetre and a fine thread.

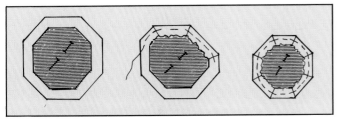

Figure 38
Preparing an English patch

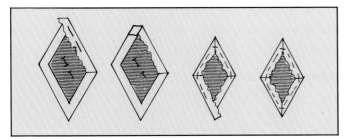

Figure 39
Turning a diamond point

If you are a purist these stitches should be made so neatly as to pick up one thread from either patch. They should also be evenly spaced and firm so that when viewed from the fabric side they are not visible. The patches must be carefully made and have a perfect geometric fit, so keep your pencil point sharp.

Materials

Templates for patchwork can be bought in a variety of shapes either in transparent or 'window' kinds. Alternatively, you will find precise instructions in Averil Colby's comprehensive book *Patchwork*. There are many books on the subject, so browse around and study the Bibliography.

While patchwork can be worked from any material, the most satisfying is cotton – which, sadly, may today mean 'polycotton', a cotton and 'Terylene' mixture which is less easy to handle than pure cotton. To join patches, use a strong cotton or similar thread. This should be fine and white for all light coloured pieces and black for the dark shades. Thicknesses will vary according to the fabric (60–100).

Sampler

This is where the exercises on shape, colour and design should help you to create an original and satisfying piece of work. Go ahead

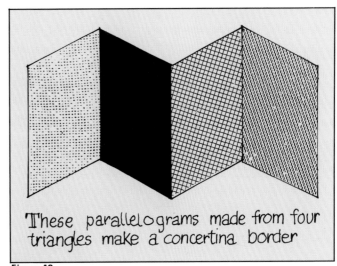

Figure 40
Concertina border

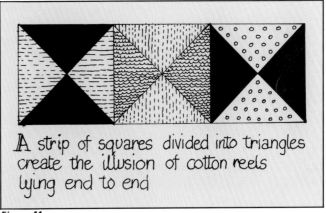

Figure 41
Cotton reels

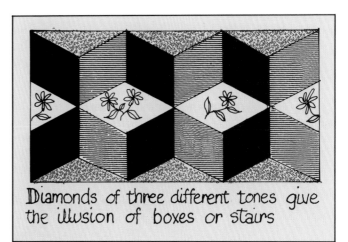

Figure 42
Tumbling boxes

and make a sampler. Avoid the temptation to mix different weights and textures of fabric. Figs 40–42 are three sketches to show how the illusion of perspective is attained.

Wrinkles

TEMPLATES: Use of a finely sharpened carpenter's pencil will always provide a fine line both to cut the paper and provide a turning line for the patch. If you make your own templates, the card will need to be firm and the pencil hard and sharply pointed. It is absolutely essential that geometric accuracy is maintained; otherwise the whole quilt will be thrown out of alignment by the accumulation of small errors. To ensure accuracy the card must be renewed when worn. A 5 mm turning is usually sufficient.

TACKING PATCHES: Never make a knot in the thread, as it will be difficult to withdraw the papers. To prevent the patches slipping, commence tacking after a corner at the first straight; when reaching a diamond point, fold the fabric up and then over. This has the same effect as a neat mitred corner. Tack the corner firmly and when you reach the last corner tack across for one stitch, remove the pin and the patch is ready to be overcast to its fellow patch.

PATTERNS: The pattern of the design in the matter of colour and balance will have been worked out beforehand. For example, a flower should be carefully placed and the curve of a leaf should be considered so that the overall design is well balanced and the eye cannot pick out the telltale misshape or inappropriate colour.

There is a set of English template patterns in the appendix and a number of books in the Bibliography. Refer to them when making your samples.

American patchwork quilts

History

Several books have been written on this subject in the last few years, and an excellent collection of the quilts themselves may be seen at Claverton Manor, the American Museum south-east of Bath.

The fundamental difference between English and American patchwork is that for English patchwork patches are laid over paper templates and whipstitched together, whereas the American shapes are joined back to back with a running stitch.

Ruth Finley's book, *Old Patchwork Quilts* (see Bibliography) lists 96 traditional patterns and 100 diagrams for working them. There are probably many more to be found.

Method

American quilts – the term does not necessarily mean that what we understand as 'quilting' has been used – are made in blocks of (usually) repetitive designs roughly 30 cm square, which are then sewn together. Having decided on the pattern to be used – there are a great many, each having a specific name – shapes are cut to suit the pattern, blending colours with care.

The Amish in America have a very distinctive and interesting use of colour which is usually dark and sombre, for example navy, brown, deep red and bottle green. The pieces are stitched together with a running stitch rather like a seam, and these then become repetitive blocks which are joined together. Once the blocks are joined, the quilt is sometimes stretched in a frame, lined with a warm fabric or wadding and quilted either simply with a running stitch or, more elaborately, to form a pattern in stitches.

Quilts were also made of lengths of plain fabric relying on the stitchery alone to form the patterns. Each design has a traditional name.

Materials

American quilts are usually made from calico.

Sampler

Choose an American design and piece together one block of a pattern. Interline it with some wadding and work a design to quilt it.

Wrinkles

American Patchwork does not use paper templates but relies on careful placing of fabric, right side back to back, and a small neat running stitch, making sure that the line is straight and equidistant from the edge of the cut shape. Unless this is observed the finished quilt will not lie reasonably flat. These quilts frequently have ruckles in them, largely because they are not made with templates.

Cathedral window patchwork (Mayflower patchwork)

History
So called since it represents stained glass windows. The origin is American or Canadian; despite its alternative name of Mayflower patchwork, it probably does not date from the Pilgrim Fathers' voyages.

Method
Cut from a plain material 15 cm squares following the grain of the material. Find the exact centre by folding and creasing with an iron if necessary. Make turnings of about 5 mm on all sides. Fold each corner to the centre point and pin in place. Fold the resulting corners to the centre and pin again, then secure the four points with a bullion knot.

Whipstitch two units together, placing right sides back-to-back. Cut out a square of contrasting material following the grain, a little smaller than the rectangle made by joining the two units together. This is an opportunity to consider colours and design. Roll the edges over to secure the coloured square. Hem down with a small running stitch.

As the material is now 'on the cross' it will roll over easily and where the edges meet you can make a neat backstitch or bullion knot. A well illustrated book on these and other forms of patchwork is *Creative Needlecraft* by Lynette de Denne.

Materials
A fine plain coloured calico and a patterned material are used.

Sampler
Make a small cushion.

Wrinkles
It is essential to keep the material on the grain and the folds correct. You should also take care to join the units accurately with right sides back-to-back. Remember that, as no lining is required and the running stitches will form a petal-like pattern on the back, you will need to work accurately on both sides. When making up the cushion use a cross-grained piece of fabric to bind the cord. Inserted into the seams, this makes a neat finish.

Log cabin patchwork

History
This was brought to Canada as an economical way of making warm coverlets. It would appear to resemble the original log cabins of rough hewn wood that were the settlers' first homes. Tradition has it that the centre patch is

Figure 43
Cathedral window

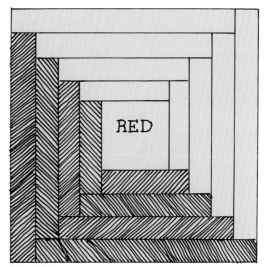

Figure 44
Log-cabin

the 'fire' and on one side the fabrics should be dark, for the men sitting in shadow, and on the other side light for the women (presumably to sew!).

Pineapple patchwork

This is a variant of log cabin in which the patch strips are laid across the four corners on the diagonal. You should make a sampler of this as well. You will find that the pattern forms a receding perspective.

Method
See Averil Colby, *Patchwork* and Lynette de Denne, *Creative Needlecraft*. Both provide excellent diagrams.

Materials
Cottons, silks, or wool – remembering that wool has a tendency to alter shape.

Sampler
Now make your own sampler of each as a useful reference.

Wrinkles
Log cabin is usually cut and marked with a sewing line. The use of polycotton gingham provides an excellent line and forms a firm backing, which, if the fabric is not to be quilted, also provides a lining for the work. Place the strips on these checks.

Figure 45
Pineapple

Random patchwork (Crazy patchwork)

History
The Victorians seem to have been very fond of this form of patchwork and much of it is still extant in the most garish colours and a variety of fabrics. It uses every last scrap of left-over fabrics.

Method
Random pieces of fabric of various textures, colours and shapes are joined edge to edge like crazy paving on a backing fabric. The joins are then feather-stitched together through both fabrics. The swing-needle sewing machine is excellent for this.

Materials
Anything goes!

Sampler
Now make your own as a useful reference.

Wrinkles
With modern iron-on interfacing it is simple to butt the uneven, or random, scraps of fabric together and this makes a backing unnecessary. A lining will be needed.

Petal patchwork

History
This seems to be a fairly modern form of patchwork. It is quick and makes warm quilts that do not need lining.

Method
Decide on the use of the fabrics – possibly the patterned one should be used for the hexagon in the centre and the plain one for the outer petals. Using your templates, cut one of each and one hexagon of wadding. (For the faint-hearted there is a diagram in the appendix but it may not be the size you require.) Place the wadding between the two shapes and; pin all three together accurately. Now turn in a hem, clipping the edge to make a semicircle, fold the 'petal' over the hexagon edges and pin it down. When sewing the edge to the hexagon choose a suitable stitch and use a quilting thread.

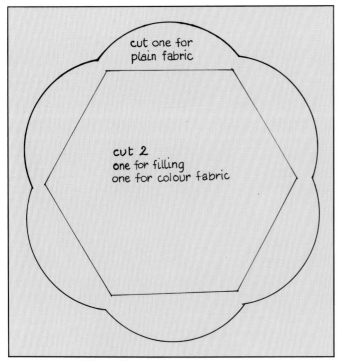

Figure 46
Petal

The centre could also be quilted.

To make up the shapes place the topside front to front, ensuring that the parts of the hexagon meet exactly, then whip-stitch the edges together as in traditional patchwork. To make a really satisfying quilt, care must be taken with the choice of colours and fabric and the patches must be made accurately. This quilt is light, warm and has no lining.

Materials
Cotton, 'Viyella', crêpe de chine and a suitably coloured cotton thread, as for quilting.

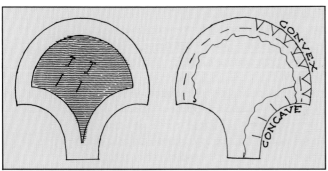

Figure 47
Clamshell

Sampler
Make a cot quilt.

Wrinkles
You should make quite sure that the centre is firmly held to the back. These quilts will withstand washing and normal wear.

Clamshell patchwork

History
This is, probably because of its shape, named after the American clam, a bi-valve shellfish similar to the scallop.

Method
Consult Averil Colby, *Patchwork*.
METHOD 1: The paper template to which the clamshell patch is attached is placed on the 'right' side of the fabric and tacked around the edge, folding the turning as flat as possible. A small clip taken out at the edge helps on the convex curve and a snip to spread the turning helps on the concave curve. The patch is then whipped to its fellow and the paper removed.
METHOD 2: The patches in clamshell can be treated differently, more as a form of appliqué. Here the paper template is tacked to the wrong side of the fabric and must be 'blind-stitched' to a base. It requires great accuracy to place each shape at 90 degrees either side by side or applied to a chequered background, but this encloses the paper and the result is stiff. Great skill is required to be successful at this form of patchwork. It is most attractive when colour and design are skilfully blended.

Materials
Fine cottons or silks, because the method involves turning a very neat fold when applying the patch.

Sampler
Make a small group of these patches and apply them to a garment.

Wrinkles
This is not an easy form of patchwork. It uses templates in two different ways. Running stitch is not used; instead the patches overlap and are either slip-stitched or hemmed. Using

The Lily Quilt Ella Pratt

thin material as a background makes it easier, although this is not absolutely necessary. Remember that, as you are dealing with curved edges, it is essential to ensure that these edges lie flat; so, when turning under the concave or convex curves of the patch, remember to snip or clip according to the shape. Use a fine slip stitch or a neat running stitch so that the shell patches, when joined, show smooth curves fitted together neatly.

To use paper templates successfully, secure each fold with a stitch over the fold. Do not use a knot because of the difficulty of removing papers.

Tack the template to the right side of the fabric, then turn the edges under (not over) and tack, again taking care to ease in the fabric.

To keep a neat point, fold over each one and tack across the fold.

Somerset patchwork (Folded patchwork)

History
This technique comes from America. It requires little sewing, as only the points are caught down.

Materials
Cotton, silk, ribbon. For the necessary accurate folding, fine fabrics work best.

Method
For your sampler cut a backing fabric 17 cm (6¾ in) square, and fold in turnings of 1 cm to form a square of 15 cm (6 in). With a transfer pencil mark out the two diagonals and note the centre of the fabric where they intersect. Now mark the vertical and horizontal halves. The measurement from the corners to the

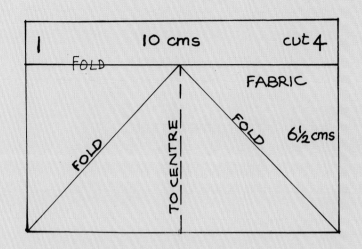

1   10 cms   cut 4

FOLD

FABRIC

FOLD   FOLD   6½ cms

TO CENTRE

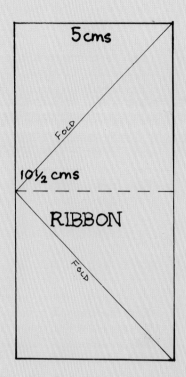

5 cms

FOLD

10½ cms

RIBBON

FOLD

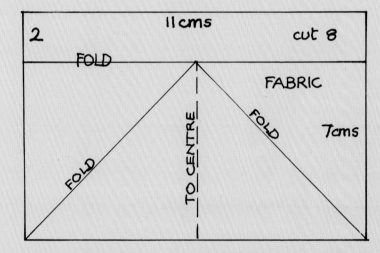

2   11 cms   cut 8

FOLD

FABRIC

FOLD   FOLD   7 cms

TO CENTRE

cut out in
firm cardboard

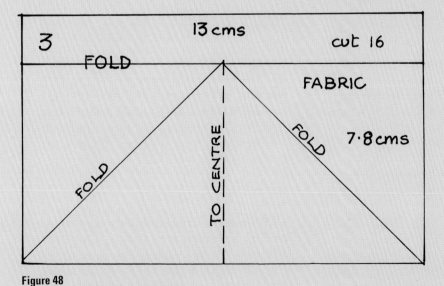

3   13 cms   cut 16

FOLD

FABRIC

FOLD   FOLD   7·8 cms

TO CENTRE

Figure 48
Templates for Somerset patchwork

central intersection should be 9 cm ($3\frac{1}{2}$ in). The appendix has a set of templates for this form of patchwork.

This is an unusual patchwork in that it requires very little stitching but the folds and points must be accurate. First cut the backing fabric. A fine calico is best because you can mark out the square to which you will work – it should measure 17 cm ($6\frac{3}{4}$ in). Fold this square vertically and horizontally to mark the exact centre, then fold again from corner to corner from each side. The line from the centre to the corner should measure 9 cm ($3\frac{1}{2}$ in). These lines will be your guide as you lay the points of the folded rectangle in place.

Cut the rectangles from the templates and, starting with the smallest template, cut four pieces of that size, fold in the hem and press. If you are using ribbon a hem would be unnecessary. Then fold in the rectangle bringing the top, folded side, down to the base; this forms an arrowhead shape and the raw edges are all concealed. Place the point exactly to the centre of the backing using the marked lines to keep an accurate placement. This uses up the four smaller folded patches.

The next size of folded patches, of which there will be eight, are placed at the folded edge: each patch is caught down with one stitch. Starting at the centre and working outwards, the number of patches increases according to the final size. Sixteen will be the next number.

It is possible to leave the parts, after the first four, free so that they can be caught back. In either case this adds interest to your design. You could keep to the original sized patch.

Use your 'window frames' or a 'circle frame' to determine the size of your final shape.

Sampler

A box top which will be determined by the size of the box, the edge being used to control the final size of the patches.

Wrinkles

Easily-folded fabrics are the most appropriate. Care should be taken with their selection to form a pleasing design. Keep the iron handy and be methodical. It is important to get the point of the folded rectangles accurately placed and to cut the fabric on the straight. The only stitching required is that to anchor the point of the fold.

Suffolk puffs (Yo yo)

History

A twentieth-century form of patchwork known in America as 'Yo yo'.

Method

Simply cut circles of fabric. Fold in and gather at the edge to form a rosette which is then filled with wool for warmth. These puffs are sewn together on the circumference to form the quilt, leaving little gaps where the circular shape prevents complete joins. Small rosettes may be bunched together to form a decoration for a garment.

Material

A soft and not too heavy fabric. When made in silk with a rich variety of colour they can be quite exquisite, very light and warm.

Sampler

Make a quilt for a doll's cot.

Wrinkles

Use a strong thread for gathering up the circle.

Seminole patchwork

History

The Seminole Indians live in the Everglades area of Florida. It is thought that they adapted American patchwork learned from white settlers, helped by the introduction of the sewing machine. The technique probably dates from the nineteenth century and uses characteristic diagonal strips of material.

Method

Set up an area of diagonal strips of material sewn together and then cut that piece of fabric into further strips across the grain of the diagonals. These are then juggled about to give the finished patchwork its distinctive pattern of stripes, chevrons or otherwise. On a piece of backing material – calico is a useful fabric for this purpose – mark out a rectangle measuring 22×17 cm $(8\frac{3}{4} \times 6\frac{3}{4}$ in$)$. The overall length should be the finished length plus the width required. Mark equal sections down both sides of the rectangle. Use a felt-tip pen to join up the markers.

For the primary set of strips, cut enough strips allowing a 12 mm ($\frac{1}{2}$ in) turning. Take the first strip with the right sides together. Pin the strips to the backing along the stitching line. Pin, sew, trim and press. Continue in this way until all the strips have been used.

For the secondary set of strips, cut strips 25 mm (1 in) wide into lengths. Cut off surplus triangles at top and bottom. Reassemble by placing right sides together and stitch 5 mm ($\frac{1}{4}$ in) seams.

To achieve a chevron effect, make two sets of strips in opposite directions which form a right angle. Make up by taking alternate strips.

Materials
Thin calico or gauze for the backing; the actual patchwork can be from any fabric that will cut and join effectively.

Sampler
A shoulder bag.

Wrinkles
The Indians used any fabric that happened to be to hand, but you may prefer to keep to one type, such as cotton or velvet. Thicker fabrics are the most difficult to use. It is not easy to create a smooth, easy to handle fabric, and it does require some ingenuity to create a lively effect.

13
Appliqué

History

Appliqué is the application of one fabric to another, or the enhancing of one fabric by applying another fabric as a pattern. It has a long history stretching back into ancient Greek and Egyptian cultures. It was also used for heraldic devices on surcoats worn to protect a man in armour against the heat, and on the trappings worn by horses. Early settlers in America took this domestic art from Europe to enliven their quilts. Today in Mongolia and Turkestan 'Yurts' have felt doors with appliqué patterns.

Method

There are several methods of applying a design: if you have cut out a flower from cretonne and want to apply it to a base fabric (known as 'lay-on', 'on-lay', or 'poor man's embroidery'), once you have tacked it firmly in place, a fine buttonhole stitch is used around the edge. The swing needle of your sewing machine in either a close satin stitch or a wider satin stitch to represent a herringbone will serve the same pupose.

A second method is to apply the cut-out fabric with a small neat straight stitch, remembering always to bring the needle up through the base fabric and down through the applied fabric. When this process is completed, couch a suitable thread around the edge hiding your stitches. This is particularly suitable for velvet, thick fabrics and leather. Remember that the grain of the material, the warp and weft must match.

When applying a thin fabric it is necessary to make a turning. As the turning should lie flat it is necessary to clip the hem line on the concave and snip it on the convex. In this way the hem folds under evenly, and should then be catch stitched or slip stitched to the base. The stitch should be very small and firm, otherwise the design will, with wear and washing, part company with the ground fabric. A decorative running stitch could also be used.

Materials

Always consider the suitability of the fabrics you intend to use. For example, it might be difficult to apply a thick fabric to a fine one, but the reverse would be simpler.

Sampler

It is necessary at all times to use a frame and also to ensure that the grain of the fabrics are correct; the cut-out pieces to be applied must lie wih the grain of the base fabric, but see 'wrinkles' below.

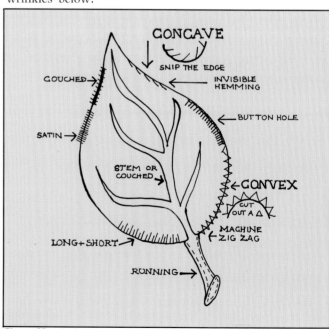

Figure 49
Appliqué

The Jack Cheryl Harris

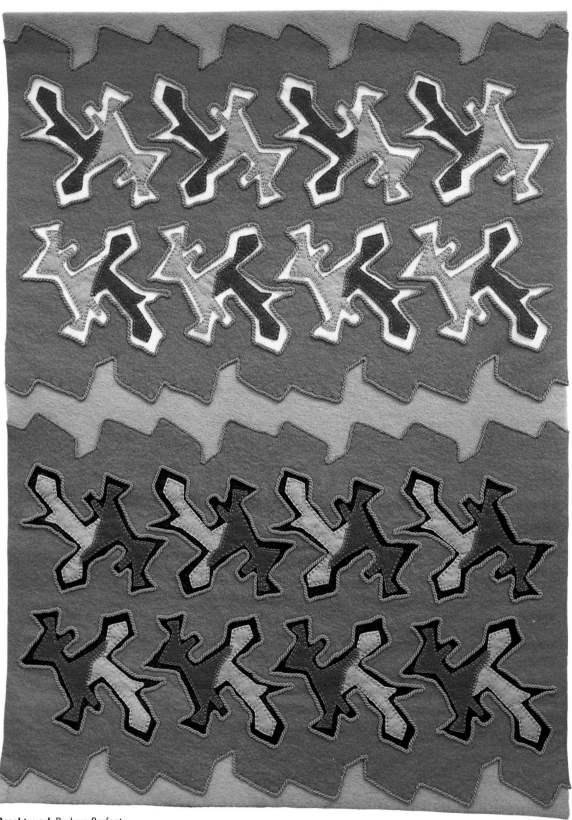

Rescht work Barbara Barfoot

Wrinkles

When applying a velvet or other fabric that frays easily, put a smear of PVA glue (this neither strings nor colours) on your finger-tip and pass this gently along the edge. This will secure the threads until you have finished applying the fabric.

When applying a pattern – say a tall lily cut from a print – to a base fabric, it is likely that the pattern will not be so obliging as to be printed with the grain of the fabric, but will, to some extent, be printed across it. Where this is so, you should endeavour to match the grains of the fabrics in the largest area – perhaps the flower head – and let the smaller areas – perhaps the stalk – find their own relationship to the base fabric grain. This is one of the reasons why it is essential to use a frame and careful firm tacking.

Reverse appliqué

History

A particular tradition is the horse cloths made of felt in south-east Europe. Rescht work (or Persian work) is another tradition discussed briefly in *The Batsford Encyclopaedia of Embroidery Techniques* by Gay Swift. See also the *Needleworker's Dictionary* by Pamela Clabburn (Macmillan).

San Blas Mola Author's collection

Method
Mary Thomas' *Dictionary of Embroidery* has an excellent introduction.

Materials
Felt.

Sampler
Use a repeat pattern for best results.

Wrinkles
Accuracy of cut is essential to make the reverse fit exactly.

San Blas

History
This method is rather like reverse appliqué and is also known as découpé. The San Blas Indians live on an island off the Pacific coast of Panama. Traditional Kuna designs such as the shark, the snake and the lion are incorporated. The Indian women add a great variety of small pieces of fabric which give their work a delightful appearance. You should not try to make it overly sophisticated because its charm would then be lost. The 'Mola' is the bodice of their costume.

Method
A number of coloured fabrics are layered on a backing of cotton; according to the design these are cut through, revealing different layers of colour which form the pattern. The cut edge is neatly folded in and slip-stitched. Sometimes a small amount of stitchery is used on the surface. The outline of the shape should not always be on one layer of colour.

Materials
Mostly cottons – although I have seen pieces of knitted fabric and even lamé used by the Indians.

Sampler
Make yourself a 'Mola' top – this is just a square of material with a dip on either side for the armhole. A very simple garment shape.

Wrinkles
Sometimes the Indians just tuck in an odd piece of fabric between the layers to improve the design.

14
Quilting

Durham and Welsh quilting

History

Quilting is another ancient technique. At a time when fabric was not so easy to come by, warm padded clothes and bedclothes were in great demand. Quilting was also used under armour to protect against chafing. If you look at the familiar English Durham and Welsh quilting, you will see the small, even stitches that outline the traditional patterns.

These patterns were cut from the templates which the men made for the womenfolk. The templates were designed for a repetitive pattern which covered the whole of the quilt.

Flat quilting is the only kind that has no interlining for warmth. It is usually made with two layers of linen using two rows of double running stitch. Research English Tudor petticoats and some foundation garments.

Method

For the traditional Durham or Welsh quilt, a sandwich of a layer of cotton, then a warm layer – probably old woollen garments cut to shape – and the top layer of cotton, were tacked together and stretched on a quilting frame ready for the design to be applied. The templates were placed on the top layer of the sandwich and the needle was used to scratch in the outline.

This transfer of the design lasted long enough for the quilter to make the outline in running stitch. When finished it was lifted from the frame, the edges turned in together, and a running stitch used to close them. Sometimes a piece of cord is covered with a fabric and inserted between the edges forming a neat finish as in upholstery, but this is not traditional.

It is sensible to learn first the 'classical'

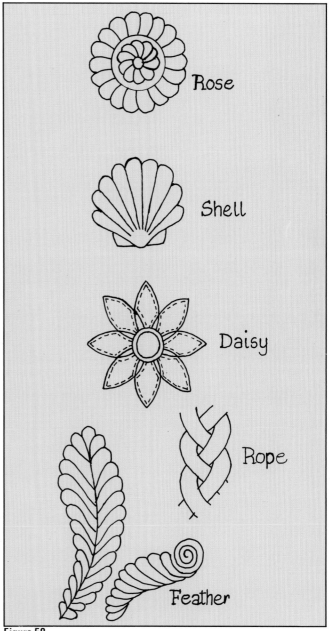

Figure 50
Old Durham and Welsh quilt templates

Rose

Shell

Daisy

Rope

Feather

method, after which you can try your own ideas. Which fabric and thread you use is for you to decide. The thread should, however, be thick enough to be seen, as this is part of the design. Mercerized threads add a soft sheen.

Materials

Modern quilt fillings are easy to care for and generally last and wash well. Traditional fillings include: cotton, kapok, wool, and sometimes old blankets and so on, in layers.

Miniature Durham quilt Elizabeth Newbery

Sampler

A bedspread.

Wrinkles

When quilting with modern fabrics, silk, or mercerized cotton, it is a good idea to use a fairly thick mercerized cotton or a perlé for silk fabric – this has the added advantage of catching the light and shade of the raised fabric. By releasing the top layer you will give a deeper appearance to the quilting. A stab stitch is also an improvement on running stitch for this type of quilting.

Italian quilting

Method

This is another variety of quilting in which the top layer of cotton, 'Viyella', silk, or satin – a fabric with a 'sheen' has an enhancing effect – is tacked to the under-layer muslin on which the design has already been placed. The stitching is in parallel lines and may be carried out in running stitch, stab stitch or by machine, working from the back of the fabric. When the whole of the design is worked, a length of soft woollen cord (Italian quilting wool is not easy to find) is threaded through between the double row of stitching, coming through the muslin at strategic intervals and leaving a small loop to prevent puckering. The design will appear in relief on the right side.

Trapunto quilting

Prepare the muslin and fabric in two layers, with the design marked on the muslin. The design is not constrained by having to be in parallel lines, but the outline must be carefully stitched. Then, in places where the design is to be padded in greater or lesser degree, make a

Glove sachet Author's collection, nineteenth century

small hole in the muslin backing and gently insert some stuffing: unspun wool or Terylene fibres are suitable. When the desired effect is reached, ladder stitch the hole together. The result will be your design in high relief on the right side.

It is also possible to sandwich a design in bright colours, possibly with felt, by placing it between two layers of fine silk, organdie or some other transparent fabric and by stitching around the outline of the 'trapped' fabric which forms the design. If you use organdie on both sides the work will be reversible.

Shadow quilting

Place the design on buckram or a similar fabric. Tack to the buckram a transparent fabric, such as muslin or organdie. With a matching or contrasting thread weave between the two layers using a herringbone stitch and being guided by the outline of the design. The design should be kept simple. On the surface there will be a neat row of stitches outlining the design and the weaving back and forth of the herringbone stitch will show through with a shadowy effect.

Cording

This is worked by trapping a cord (such as a piece of upholstery cord) behind the top fabric with a herringbone stitch which passes through the fabric and behind the cord. It is easier to work by tacking a firm backing of buckram or thick paper which prevents the needle passing into the backing but allows it to trap the cord. This form of quilting must be lined. Note that cord quilting can also be done on a zigzag sewing machine.

Samplers

As each form of quilting differs, you will want to carry out separate samplers for each. For corded quilting: your signature; for trapunto: a waistcoat; for shadow quilting: a cushion.

Wrinkles

All these quiltings are better carried out in a frame which helps to keep the sandwich in position and prevents the cords and stuffings from distorting either the design or the fabrics. Remember: when making a garment, you must allow for shrinking as the quilting progresses. If you use a sewing machine, remember that the frame will need to be upside down to keep the fabric taut and close to the bobbin plate. The foot has to be removed to free the needle to follow the design. Don't forget to lower the pressure foot.

Safety first

Use a darning foot to act as a needle guard and keep your fingers well away from the needle and refer to page 83 for sewing machine safety notes.

15
Machine embroidery

History

The earliest known sewing machine was invented by Thomas Saint in 1790 and was designed to sew leather. Walter Hunt invented the first lock-stitch machine in 1834. It was the first to have the mechanism for machine embroidery. The first really practical machine was developed by Isaac Singer in August 1851. Thereafter machine embroidery developed rapidly and began to compete with hand embroidery.

In the late 1920s the sewing machine was used for creative embroidery, and in the second half of the century many people have made advances using the modern swing-needle machines so that the sewing machine is now an accepted part of mainstream embroidery.

Study the work of Dorothy Benson, who did so much to interpret this form of decorative art for the Singer Sewing Machine Company, and read Joan Edwards' book on her. Books in the Bibliography will give you a good introduction to the use of the modern machine and the development of modern machine embroidery.

Sampler

For your sampler, see how many hand techniques you can successfully produce with the swing needle machine. You should experiment on a variety of fabrics, including soluble fabrics used in machine lacemaking. Make full use of books in the Bibliography.

Wrinkles

It is essential to use a circular frame with a low rim. Some useful metal or plastic clip-in frames can be obtained for this purpose, but may not grip the material as well as a cloth-bound wooden frame. Having placed your design on the fabric, put the fabric into the frame so that it is absolutely drum-tight. If you use a wooden tambour frame, the surface you wish to work on should be on the 'inside' of the frame within the rings so that the machine foot can exert pressure between the fabric and the bobbin plate if required. This is the reverse of the usual way of using this frame; once the foot lever is in the down position, as it always must be, the needle is unable to drag the fabric up and down as it passes through.

Preparing the frame

To prepare your frame, bind the inner ring with tape (lampshade frame binding tape works well): this will prevent slipping, accommodate most fabrics, particularly the loosely woven, and ensure that the frame is smooth and will not harm silk or other fine fabrics.

Place the outer ring on a firm flat surface

Safety: some very important points

Always use some foot – a darning foot if at all possible – to guard your fingers from the needle. It is essential for safety's sake to keep both your hands away from the unguarded needle – clear outside the frame – and to use a wooden cocktail stick to do any necessary manoeuvring of the work within the frame. The typical accident happens when the operator has not used pins and tacking to hold securely the fabric to be applied. It only takes a quick, thoughtless dart of the fingers near to the needle for you to be in deep, and very painful, trouble. Should this happen, despite all precautions, always remove the needle from the machine – and not from your hand – and take it and the thread with you to hospital.

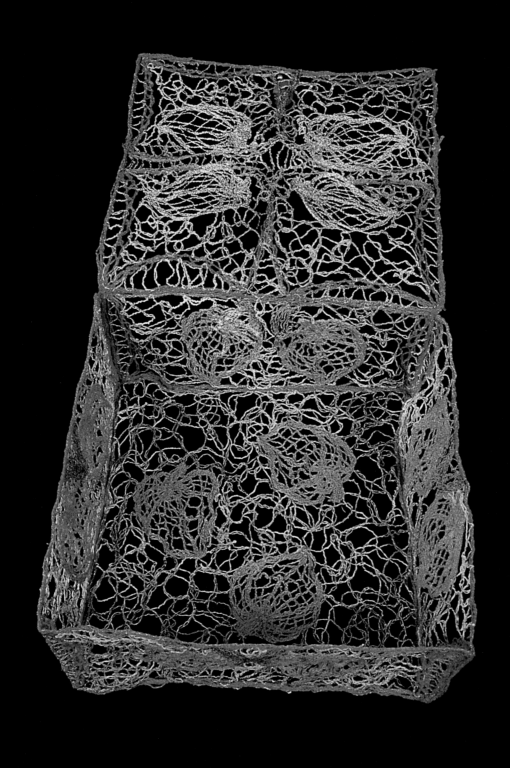
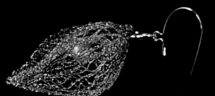
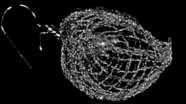

with the screw slightly loose to accommodate the inner ring and your fabric easily. Taking care to have the grain of the fabric straight and your design already on your fabric, place the fabric over the outer ring. Now press the inner ring into the outer, so trapping the fabric. It is essential to be certain that the fabric is taut and that the grain is undistorted. The frame should only be tightened fully when you are absolutely satisfied with the fabric's positioning. Do not try to reposition the fabric when the frame is tightened up fully – loosen it off a little first.

If you do not use great care at this stage, problems that will occur are: gaps in your stitches, puckering, and an overall distortion of the finished work. The fabric should be drum-tight.

Preparing the machine

The foot and teeth
Prepare your machine by removing the presser foot and its securing screw and by lowering the teeth. If you have an old machine which does not allow you to drop the teeth, you can make a protective card or slip of stiff plastic, using the metal plate as a template.

Bottom spool tension
Prepare the bottom spool tension for whatever thread you are using by adjusting the tiny grub screw at the side of the shuttle or spool carrier. Always turn it in – or out – by half or quarter turns with the correctly sized screwdriver and note down what you are doing as you go – so that if you have to dash for the milk saucepan, then you will not get lost! Do this operation over a soft cloth, deep tray or the lid of a box so that if the screw drops out you will be able to retrieve it easily. Without it the machine is useless, and sometimes it can be extraordinarily difficult to get new ones, even from the agents for your machine. You have been warned: take great care not to lose it.

The correct tension for any particular thread will be approximately correct if the thread, properly inserted, will only just support the weight of the spool in its case, without unwinding.

Threading
Thread the needle and spool with machine cotton thread. Don't use the more expensive threads until you really understand your machine and the tension adjustments. Now place your prepared frame under the needle, lower the presser bar and the darning foot. The machine will not apply tension to the upper thread unless the bar is lowered.

Forming the first stitch
It is very important to ensure that the first stitch is properly formed through a single needle hole. Your first stitch needs to be made where you intend to start your embroidery. Hold the end of the top thread in your left hand while gently turning the machine mechanism through one cycle to bring the lower thread up through the fabric so that the needle is now clear of the fabric. Hold the two threads in your left hand and place both hands on the frame edge.

Stitching
Now start to doodle and practise using your machine. Begin slowly and only gradually increase your speed. There are three basic stitches with which you should already be familiar. The zigzag stitch facility on the machine may be used densely as satin stitch or less densely according to need for buttonhole or appliqué. If you have a modern swing-needle machine, satin stitch is easily adjusted; but if you are using a machine with no 'zigzag' then you will have to move your frame from side to side to obtain satin stitch.

Whip stitch

This is a decorative corded stitch which provides density of colour and varies the texture. In the bobbin use a fine machine embroidery thread, or else a fine silk. Thread the needle with a thicker thread according to the texture you are looking for. Only experimentation will teach you the proper balance of the threads and when to place the thicker thread in the bobbin and work upside down. The bobbin tension should be loose.

Run the machine fast, but move the frame slowly so that the loose bobbin thread will whip round the tight top thread, thus giving a corded appearance.

Very attractive effects are produced by varying the tension.

Feather stitch

This is a variety of whip stitch. The threads you use will be similar; the top tension needs to be as tight as possible short of breaking the thread while the bobbin tension is as loose as possible while maintaining a slight resistance to prevent loops forming. As always, your fabric must be tight and firm in the frame. The feathered effect is produced by the tight top thread pulling the looser bobbin thread through the fabric. Run the machine more slowly than for whip stitch, but work the frame in quick, circular movements.

Cable stitch

This stitch is used to handle those threads which will not run through the needle and must be used from the bobbin instead. Threads which are thicker, fluffier, hairy, uneven or slubby, decorative threads, fine ribbons and threads which contain 'Lurex' or other metallized finishes will normally not be used on the needle or top side of the machine, and will need to be hand wound on the bobbin for use if necessary.

Since the fabric is worked from the back, you will have to remember that your design, which will have to be visible to you looking at the 'wrong' side of the fabric, must be reversed.

Experiment by varying the top and bottom threads, the tensions and the density of the stitch by running the machine at different speeds and manipulating the frame accordingly.

Wrinkles

Always keep fingers away from the needle – use a cocktail stick to manipulate any stray threads. Always use an effective method to avoid losing the tiny tension adjuster grub screw on the bottom spool. This will save you endless grief and misery.

'Oddball' threads are useful, but may mean that not many yards can be stored on the bobbin, so you will need to design for a larger number of starts and stops. Where these come in awkward places, it is a good idea to use either a stiletto or a tapestry needle to pierce a small hole to bring the thread through to the back. Take care that the resulting hole does not distort the fabric, and twist the top and bottom thread ends together to make for a freer passage. Snip the larger threads off with care, as it is unsightly to have great tufts of thread ends behind the work.

When using thread that cannot be put on the bottom spool for couching, work from the right side of your fabric and – using all the skill at your command – gently feed the wool on the fabric, couching as you go, and guiding it with the cocktail stick.

To prevent the drag which occurs when you alter the direction of your sewing, mark time for a few stitches before moving off in the new direction. Remember that it may be necessary to change the colour of the needle thread to prevent any blurring of the design on the 'right' side of the fabric.

Machine appliqué

Because it is so necessary to keep the tension and grain of your two fabrics constant – as well as to keep the fingers well out of the danger area around the needle while stitching – it is wise to place both the background fabric and the fabric to be applied into your frame together.

To avoid marking a delicate fabric, place your design – drawn on a sheet of tissue or tracing paper – into the frame as well as the fabrics. Transfer the design with the needle in straight stitch. Remove it from the frame and tear off the paper. Cut closely, but carefully, around the applied fabric and return to the frame. Then do any decorative stitching you may wish to use to fasten the edges securely and hide, where necessary, the original straight stitch, which is, after all, only the tacking together of the ground and applied fabrics.

Where only a small piece of fabric is available, thoroughly baste the appliqué fabric to the background, or use 'Bondaweb'. These methods – if carefully carried out – should avoid puckering and distortions.

Detached machine appliqué

A great advantage of machine embroidery is the ease of attaching free-standing pieces. These are made by the usual machine appliqué method: the fabric is placed with the design in the frame, the machine is used to apply a close zigzag all around the shape as in buttonhole stitch, and the shape required is then cut from the base fabric as closely as possible along the edge of the stitching. The resulting shape will have a slightly greater stiffness than the original fabric, which allows it to be used free-standing.

The method permits you to alter the stiffness or softness of the shape as you wish by adding more stitching or an extra layer of fabric.

Village pump Joy Alderson

Reverse machine appliqué

This is similar to ordinary appliqué, except that the two layers of fabric are cut away after stitching to leave only a single layer. Start with the background fabric uppermost. Use a straight stitch to set the layers together; then, after trimming away the excess fabric inside the line, stitch again using zigzag stitch to maintain the edge. Finally trim away the fabric outside the stitching at the back.

Applied threads

When you wish to use threads that are too thick, textured or harsh to be threaded through the needle or wound on the bobbin, then you can couch them on the fabric. Unless the fabric is very stable you will need to use a frame, and it is best to set the thread with tacking before you attempt to couch it. Use a cocktail stick – not a needle – to hold the thread in position and to keep your fingers far away from the machine needle. To produce a pile effect use the cocktail stick to lift the thread as you couch it down and cut the thread to raise the pile.

Use either a straight or zigzag stitch – the latter will show more of the thread to be couched once the lower thread has been pulled through and a few straight stitches made. When filling a space work from the outside inwards.

Only by your own experiments will you find your way through the many effects you can produce. Scrim – because of its loose and uneven weave – is an exciting fabric under the machine needle and will produce openwork, cutwork, and lace effects. The books in the Bibliography will help you to explore these stitches in their own right.

Eyelets

Use the eyelet plate for your machine and a small frame so that the whole thing can be easily rotated under the machine arm. On the surface of the eyelet plate is a small post with a slot for the swing needle to stitch through. In essence you are working a zigzag stitch around the hole you cut for eyelet by pivoting the fabric in the frame around the pivot-post on the plate.

Use a sharp stiletto to make the holes in the fabric and take care not to cut through more threads than you absolutely have to. Note that the needle must be unscrewed to permit the frame and the fabric to be placed over the pivot-post.

Large eyelets

To make a larger eyelet hole, draw a circle to outline the size of the eyelet required. Run a few rows of very fine straight stitching around the circle to strengthen it and to keep the fabric from stretching. Cut out the fabric in the centre of the hole, and then use the pivot-post as a guide to keep the zigzag stitching to the edge of the hole.

Other eyelets

A wide variety of different edge effects can be obtained by using the free-running setting, straight stitches, and different stitch patterns in combination.

Important safety notes on the use of acetone

Acetone and its vapour are toxic and highly inflammable. Like all vaporous materials you should avoid breathing it in. If you can smell it you are breathing it, so for your own safety, make sure that you are working in a very well ventilated room or preferably in the open air and up wind from the chemical.

Never smoke near any inflammable vapour – this seems obvious, until someone forgets and the accident happens.

Acetone will dissolve many plastics, so you should always use a glass, ceramic or metal dish and use only as much acetone as will just cover the piece.

You should never handle acetone with bare skin, so use a pair of tweezers to handle the piece. Use suitable gloves and eye protection.

Never pour the remaining acetone down the sink. The dissolved fabric will go solid and block the drain. If only slightly used the remainder may be kept – preferably in a metal container and always with an airtight lid. Otherwise let it evaporate in a safe place along with the remainder on the fabric and then throw the remaining skin into the dustbin.

Dissolved fabric work

This approach uses pure acetate fabric – which dissolves easily in acetone – as a temporary support for thread stitching. Acetate fabric is normally used to line silk and other soft fabrics. After the stitching has been completed, the base acetate is dissolved away in a bath of acetone, leaving a lace-like fabric. It is essential to use either pure cotton or silk thread. Machine embroidery 50 is good for fine work.

Remember that the design – and the stitching – must be linked everywhere, otherwise the stitching will be shapeless when the acetate is dissolved away. Use close stitches, either straight or zigzag, and remember to link all elements of the design together keeping the edges really neat.

Set up for normal machine embroidery with the acetate framed before the design is traced on it. Trim the fabric as far as possible before placing it in the acetone.

There are other fabrics (often very hard to find, even in specialist shops) which dissolve: one in cold water, the other in hot water; you must remember that the merest hint of water – even a sneeze! – will make these delicate fabrics dissolve. The least successful fabric, in my experience, is dissolving muslin. This is not unlike stiffened cheesecloth and requires a hot iron to dissolve it away after embroidery. This has pitfalls with many fabrics and threads that are unable to take a hot iron.

16
From design to fabric

This chapter is about converting your designs into an embroidery. Now that you have mastered the basic stitches and techniques as well as the essentials of developing a design, it is time to try your skills out by combining them to make an embroidery.

Take the subjects in rotation. Use an A3 size sheet of paper and make your design in whichever medium you think is appropriate to the exercise. Remember that you should specify the design in terms of fabric, thread, colour and stitchery, giving a good impression of the techniques involved and the rationale behind the design.

You should write a letter presenting your submission. Indicate the ways in which your design meets the requested commission and include clips of the fabrics and threads you intend to use, the cost of the materials and of your time in executing the commission.

This set of twelve exercises has been chosen to encourage you to look in detail at the technical problems which arise in meeting someone else's requirements and to present your solution in a coherent fashion.

---

1. A set of table mats
(Two large, 40 × 30 cm (16 × 12 in) and six small, 30 × 20 cm (12 × 8 in)
Some points to remember:
Avoid placing your design where it will be obscured by the plate. Is it to be geometric, symbolic or realistic? Remember the problems of scale in your design. Try to make the design appropriate to its use by considering washability, heat insulation and sophistication (linen, cotton, tweedy wool).

2. A set of beach wear for a young woman
Some points to remember:
Large and small towels, bag, swimsuit and/or bikini, shoes and changing wrap. Brilliant colours which should be sun, seawater and wash-fast, a waterproof bag to hold wet things, plimsolls or rope-soled shoes (towelling, stretch materials).

3. Panel for a teenager's bedroom, 100 × 50 cm (40 × 20 in)
Some points to remember:
The teenager is suspicious of the project. High fashion (research this) – latest trends but with a stylish quality to avoid a throw-away ethic. Include references to the teenager's interests. A background material such as strong calico would make a good base for your design. Appliqué and quilting; you could apply actual objects such as wheels, springs, tapes, bones.

4. Frieze for a children's hospital ward, 250 × 100 cm (100 × 40 in)
Some points to remember:
Impressions of popular stories from television and radio; traditional nursery rhymes – this might be interpreted using a large metal mesh. It is possible to appliqué other materials to canvas and to paint it as well. You should consider hygiene, acoustics and fire resistance when selecting materials. The senior ward sister is fierce and the cleaners are underpaid.

5. An architect has commissioned a hanging for the foyer of an electronics factory, 200 × 175 cm (80 × 70 in)
Some points to remember:
You are required to 'interpret the humanity of electronics and electronic machinery'. The managing director's wife is involved and her taste in colour is, well, 'eccentric'. Some light-

Sparrow in a blackberry bush Sereta Thompson ▶

emitting diodes and other electronic bits and pieces may be available through a friendly marketing executive.

6. Commission for a hanging to reduce noise in a new factory canteen, 250×600 cm (100×240 in)

Some points to remember:

The canteen is used by staff at all levels in the new factory. Acoustics, easy cleaning and non-retention of food odours; expression of the new development in company-employee relationships is expected. There is a strong lobby for making the rather naked ducts and drains of the building more acceptable without hiding them completely. The foreign management has influence.

7. Hanging for a health studio, $175 \times 100 \times 75$ cm ($70 \times 40 \times 30$ in)

Some points to remember:

Soft sculpture – should you parody a body-cult atmosphere? The hanging must be mobile and not be in the way.

8. You are asked to furnish a garden centre shop

Some points to remember:

Your brief is to design curtains, chair covers, blinds against the heat of the sun for picture windows, facia panels for the tops of display cases and racks, signs and similar items.

9. You want to make a presentation box for a friend on an important occasion

Some points to remember:

The design should relate to the shape of the box – whether it is square, round, hexagonal or polygonal. The embroidery should be in some way expressive of the occasion. A free-standing bouquet of flowers might be included. Some soft sculpture may be appropriate. Attention should be given to the way in which the box is to be displayed. Continuity of design between inside and outside should be preserved.

10. You want to make a cover for an elaborate nineteenth-century iron bed with brass knobs

Some points to remember:

The client expressly asks that it should be modern and abstract. Some form of quilted patchwork in a non-traditional style is sought. The design may include areas of appliqué. The bedroom is predominantly a soft pale yellow and the cover is to use bright yellow tints. Your client particularly admires the design of the bed's frame ends and the knobs.

11. A costume for a pantomime

Some points to remember:

The costume will have to make an impact from a distance and be suitably overstated. This is a chance to use some very exciting fabrics – look in the jumble sale, the dressing-up box, and the market. Cost is to be minimal.

12. Running water

Some points to remember:

Reflections, wetness, motion, spray, eddies.

Two embroideries with quite different purposes should be studied in connection with your own projects:

The Bayeux Tapestry
Embroidered, probably in Canterbury, to hang on the walls of Bishop Odo's church in Bayeux, Normandy. Eleventh century. Bayeux Tapestry Museum, Normandy, France.

William Morris
Embroidered Panel for the Red House circa 1860. The Victoria and Albert Museum, London.

General advice

Design first, then assemble all your fabrics and threads including anything you may wish to use, such as shells, sequins, and metal objects, before commencing the practical work. It is frustrating to begin and then find progress held up unnecessarily.

Remember to keep that facility for sketching that you should be developing by drawing in your sketchbook for 20 minutes each day.

17
Christian ecclesiastical embroidery

The Christian traditions

Some of the Christian Churches with special embroidery traditions that should be considered are:

Anglican (England)
Coptic (Egypt, Ethiopia)
Episcopalian (USA)
Greek Orthodox
Roman Catholic
Russian Orthodox

All these traditions tell the story of the Christian faith in pictorial and symbolic forms. Embroidery, stained glass, sculpture and frescos have all been used to enhance and emphasize the teachings of these churches. We are concerned with the actual embroidery of vestments and church furnishings. Modern embroidery designers have largely freed themselves from the most stultifying of the design conventions in this field and today ecclesiastical work is as fertile a field for ideas as any.

Many of the articles mentioned in this chapter are not always used by every community and some have been discarded quite deliberately because they are of no present use. The student, faced with identifying or restoring them will, however, need to know their names and uses.

Opus Anglicanum

The famous school of embroidery in England known as *Opus Anglicanum* flourished from the twelfth to the fourteenth century. It was originally based on Byzantine textiles imported from south-eastern Europe. There are mounted fragments of this earlier work from St Cuthbert's Stole (*c*. AD 905–10) in Durham Cathedral, England.

Designs were in the same tradition as frescos

PRIEST ROBED
drawn from a brass rubbing

Figure 51

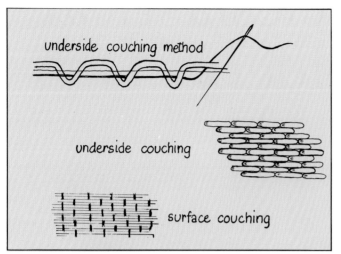

Figure 52
Couching

relating a story in a stylized manner. Mostly worked by men, they were often exported as gifts between the nobility and senior churchmen.

The unique underside couching of the gold is an important reason for the longevity of these embroideries, since while the gold thread lay on the top of the fabric, the threads used to couch it were drawn down into the underlying fabric and were not exposed to wear.

Distinguishing features of *Opus Anglicanum* are the huge eyes, the large heads and the hands that are all delicately embroidered. You should study the Syon Cope (described in Chapter 20), which is in the Victoria and Albert Museum, London. *Opus Anglicanum* eventually had a wide influence all over Europe, although with the advent of the Black Death in the fourteenth century it faded out.

The Reformation brought to England the destruction of many vestments and furnishings. Some were successfully hidden from the worst vandalism, and examples have sometimes been found folded into hassocks and in similar places. Pieces may still be seen at the Vatican in Rome and at the Victoria and Albert Museum, London – mostly ecclesiastical vestments and furnishings.

Stitches typical of *Opus Anglicanum* are: split stitch, long and short stitch, plain couching and metal thread work, mounted jewels, and raised work. It was carried out on handspun and woven linen and the embroidery threads

used were mostly silk. After the advent of the Black Death the work never really reached the same technical standard.

In 1963 the British Arts Council held an exhibition of *Opus Anglicanum* at the Victoria and Albert Museum in London and gathered there some 160 pieces. You should refer to studies by A. F. Kendrick (*English Embroidery*, Batsford, 1904), Mrs Archibald Christie (*English Mediaeval Embroidery*, Oxford University Press, 1938), Professor Talbot Rice (*English Art 871–1100*, Oxford University Press, 1952), Beryl Dean (*Ecclesiastical Embroidery*, 1989, and *Embroidery for Religion and Ceremonial*, 1986, both Batsford) see Bibliography.

Or Nué

This technique, also known as Burgundian embroidery, Italian shading and glaze stitch, uses a contrasting couching thread to trace a pattern on laid gold thread using different spacings and densities of couching to build up the picture or pattern required. The technique

Celtic Cross – detail of Treleigh frontal Sereta Thompson

reached its finest flowering in Burgundy, France in the fourteenth and fifteenth centuries.

The word 'nué' comes from the French for 'cloud', as in storm cloud or a cloud of insects.

The whole surface of the work is covered in gold with the pattern oversewn in coloured threads. The design is traced out by spacing the thread to give a gradation of colour and of the amount of gold thread allowed to show.

Refer to *Ecclesiastical Embroidery* by Beryl Dean, who has also some excellent guidance for ceremonial work (see Bibliography).

Varieties of embroidery within the traditions

Many of the illustrations in this chapter are of pieces from the set of teaching aids for ecclesiastical embroidery worked by Jeanette Morton, for which she made a storage box which serves as the altar and has drawers in the back.

Linen and vestments

There are several distinct forms of embroidery used by the Anglican, Episcopalian, Roman Catholic and Orthodox Churches.

The altar linen, and the white linen under-vestments worn by the priest and his assistants include:

Altar	Under-vestments
Corporal	Alb
Credence cloth	Amice
Fair linen cloth	Cotta
Lavabo towel	Girdle
Pall	Rochet
Purificator	Surplice

Today 'white' can include shades of cream and grey. Sometimes the Alb and the Amice can be decorated with a panel of embroidery called an Apparel – see below under 'Vesting the priest and his assistants'. The outer garments, by tradition, are worn to add colour and lustre to the Holy Communion service or Mass, especially at major festivals. They have come down to us from the everyday clothes of the people of the early church.

Outer vestments include:

Chasuble	Hood	Stole
Cope	Maniple	Tunicle
Dalmatic	Mitre	

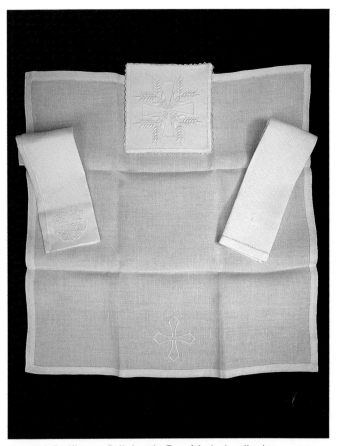

Corporal, Purificator, Pall, Lavabo Towel Author's collection

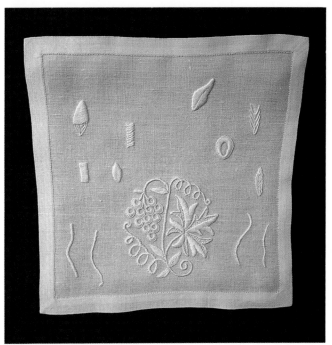

Linen sampler Author's collection

Like the altar furnishings, some are lavish in their use of silks and metal threads and some are simple – even plain – relying on the many different fabrics and threads available today.

Furnishings

The furnishings, including the Altar Frontal, Pulpit Fall, the Dossal Curtains, the Burse and Veil and the Banners, are generally worked in a different style of embroidery. Do not forget the kneelers – normally worked in counted thread on canvas.

Falls

Lecterns and Pulpit Falls follow the seasonal colours and the symbolism of the liturgy or the dedication of the building.

Banners

These are carried at the head of processions and lead such organizations as the Choir, the childrens' Sunday School and the Mothers' Union. They also follow the symbolism of the organization they represent.

Kneelers and cushions

These are usually made in canvas work, and careful designing by an expert to keep them uniform and appropriate is very necessary.

Vesting the altar

To 'vest' the altar, a thickish felt cut as a template is first placed over the top; some altars are of stone and it is necessary to have a material that will resist damp and give a slight padding. Next place over the felt a length of white linen or cotton the same shape. The Fair Linen Cloth will measure two thirds of the

Evenweave linen sampler Author's collection

Fine linen sampler Author's collection

distance between the floor and the altar table in length, and in width be measured from edge to edge.

When there is no Communion service, a two-part dust cover made of some suitable linen or cotton in an appropriate colour is used – one part is the width of the candle holder bases and the other wide enough to cover the remaining length and width of the Fair Linen Cloth. The latter is removed for a celebration of Holy Communion. The purpose of this dust cover is to keep the Fair Linen Cloth fresh and clean. Poor practice is to clean the brasses and silver *in situ* and to attend to the flowers in like manner. The altar is never the proper place for these operations.

Fair Linen Cloth

The only essential embroideries are the five crosses – a small one at each corner and a larger one in the centre. A rough measurement would be four at 5 cm (2 in) and one at 7 cm ($2\frac{3}{4}$ in). These crosses represent the dedication of the altar – similar crosses may be seen incised in the top – and symbolize the five wounds of Christ.

The hems should be hem stitched, and the edges hemmed by hand. It may be possible to buy linen of the correct width but the selvedge must be removed (keep this selvedge, which is rather like tape and makes excellent frame-binding material).

The embroidery is placed on the two ends of the cloth above the hem and below the end of the altar. Usually the thread matches the fabric, but on some Continental cloths you may see black embroidery on a grey fabric and sometimes red or blue embroidery used on a white or cream fabric. Any embroidery that will tolerate the rigours of frequent washing and ironing is suitable. For this reason drawn threads and needleweaving should not be too deep. Broderie Anglaise, skillfully handled, is quite suitable.

No other embroidery should be worked on the altar top and the crosses themselves should not be raised work as the chalice must not tilt nor spill. The two hems of the cloth should have a double hem about 7 cm or 8 cm ($2\frac{3}{4}$–3 in) deep and this should be turned up twice – a double hem of this kind gives just

enough weight to make the cloth hang correctly. Some cloths have crochet lace added, which serves the same purpose, but it is not necessary and it does create problems when laundering. There is a note on laundering care at the end of this section.

Burse and Veil

The Burse and Chalice Veil are part of the Eucharistic vestments and follow the liturgical colours. The embroidery is usually symbolic or refers to the saint to whom the church is dedicated. The Veil is about 50 cm (20 in) square and the Burse, which resembles the covers of a book, is 20 cm (8 in) square. The Veil covers the Chalice and Paten and the Burse, which is really a pocket, holds the Corporal and is placed on the top. The embroidery will match the Veil. The Veil should never be folded, but spread flat or rolled on a cardboard tube with acid-free tissue. The Burse should be folded in similar paper.

Corporal

This is a small cloth laid under the Communion vessels. It measures 40 cm (16 in) square with a narrow hem and mitred corners; it is folded 3×3 which gives nine squares. In the central bottom square embroider a cross to match the large cross on the Fair Linen Cloth. The Corporal is kept inside the Burse.

The Pall

This is a stiffened square measuring between 10 cm (4 in) and 15 cm (6 in) according to the size of the Paten (a dish which fits over the Chalice) that it is to cover. It is embroidered on the top side. Usually this embroidery has some symbolism such as an ornate cross, or a 'Pelican in her Piety', a ship, fishes, and the emblem of the church for which the set of altar linen is destined.

White card is used to stiffen the Pall which can be made up in a variety of ways. The envelope method is preferable, as this facilitates laundering; but some sew the card in and at the four corners place a narrow tape or elastic into which is inserted a square of linen, cotton or blotting paper. These can be removed and destroyed after each celebration.

Burse and veil in Sarum red, St Mary's, Walditch

The edge of the Pall quickly becomes worn and to avoid extra wear a row of needle-made lace can be worked directly on the linen. This lace is made in buttonhole stitch over evenly-spaced threads. A second row looping the previous row may be added.

The Purificator
This is the fine linen square measuring about 20 cm (8 in) according to the size of the chalice) and folded in three. A cross is embroidered in one corner. For guidance on the making and embroidery refer to the previous paragraphs. The Purificator is used to clean and dry the vessels after use.

Lavabo Towel
A narrow strip of linen – preferably Hucka-back – folded in three with a cross at the base of the centre fold; the same style of embroidery applies. The towel is used by the Priest when he washes his hands.

The Credence Cloth
The vessels including the cruet of wine and water and the wafer box are placed on the Credence Table as well as the basin and ewer. The Credence Cloth is made to the measurements of the Credence Table which may be only a stone niche in the wall of the Sanctuary. The preparation and treatment should follow that of the Fair Linen Cloth.

Altar Frontals
There are two kinds. The Tabard covers the front of the altar only; it may be on a frame hooked to the altar or attached to a length of fabric which covers the altar top and hangs down about one third at the back of the altar with a heavy rod through the hem at the back to hold it in place. The Superfrontal – a narrow strip of embroidered fabric running the length of the altar – is attached to this piece of fabric and hangs over the top edge of the Altar Frontal.

The Laudian, or throw-over Altar Cloth, is, as the name implies, a large piece of fabric that covers the altar, hanging down all round to envelop the whole of the altar.

Embroideries for these two frontals must be different in style to cope with their shapes. For example, a Laudian style needs a central motif design, while the Tabard frontal and Super-frontal may be embroidered over the whole of their area.

Sometimes in the past Altar Frontals were divided with Orphreys (bands of embroidery covering the seam) because the cloth was not

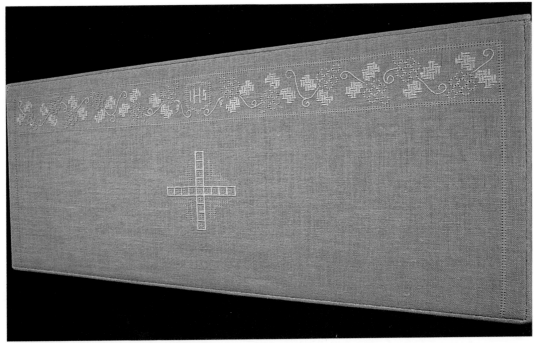

Altar Frontal – teaching aid Jeanette Morton

The drawers behind the altar Jeanette Morton

woven wide enough to make one seamless piece.

Another matter to consider is the distance at which the frontals are seen. Small fussy detail is inappropriate, but the overall design for a complete set must take into account the size of the Burse and Veil, also the Priest's vestments. Not every design will reduce or enlarge satisfactorily. The shape of the Offertory Bags also needs to be considered.

Fair Linen Cloth – teaching aid Jeanette Morton

Vesting the Priest and his assistants

Beneath the embroidered outer vestments the following linen vestments are worn:

Alb
A white Cassock, often with a hood. Today the black serge Cassock is not usually worn under vestments during the Holy Communion service, and the Alb has taken its place.

Amice
A large square of linen 1 m (1 yard) square. At one edge is an 'Apparel' which is a strip of embroidery measuring 20 by 8 cm ($8 \times 3\frac{1}{4}$ in). Tapes 2 m (2 yards) long are attached at the top corners. These are used to tie the Amice over the shoulders and around the waist. The Amice covers the head when robing. Where the new white Alb is worn, the hood replaces the Amice.

The Apparel
This is a short length of embroidery found on the Amice and at the lower end of the Alb; originally it may have been intended to resist wear and tear.

The Priest with Alb and Stole Jeanette Morton ▶

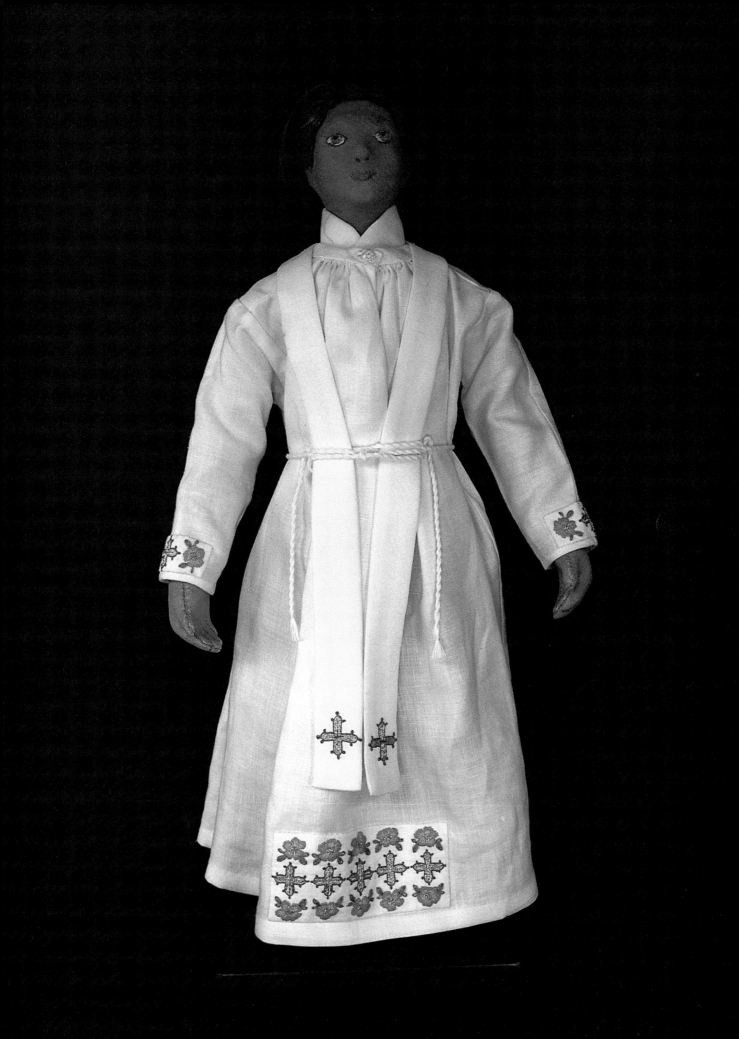

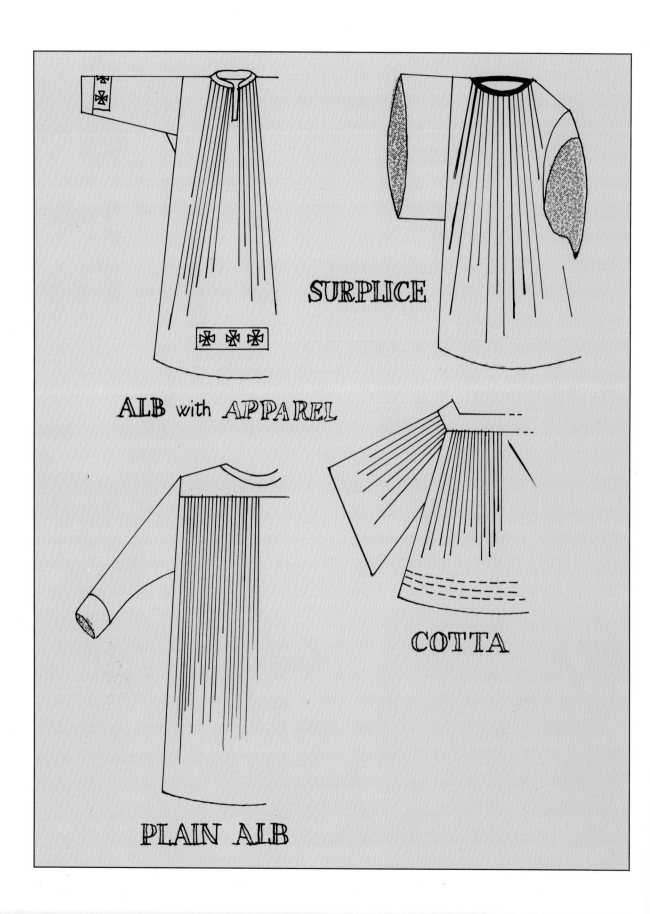

SURPLICE

ALB with APPAREL

COTTA

PLAIN ALB

AMICE

DALMATIC (Deacon)

Clavi

TUNICLE (Sub-Deacon)

Outer garments carrying richer decoration

Stole
This is the one vestment without which no sacrament should be celebrated. It therefore has a very special place. Though stoles may be made in varying widths according to fashion and fancy, a width of 5 cm (2 in) at the nape of the neck widening to 10 cm (4 in) at the base is the most usual. There is always a cross at the nape of the neck. A small piece of lace is sewn over this cross to prevent dirt and wear because it can be removed for laundering. The two ends are usually more lavishly embroidered. The stole is caught back in a loop of the cord around the waist before the Chasuble is put on.

Chasuble
There are two styles in current use: the Gothic and the Roman, or 'Fiddleback'. The Gothic comes right down over the forearms in a free-flowing straight line from the neck. The Roman is more cut away, usually stiff, and normally tied with tapes underneath at the front.

Today the embroiderer has moved away from the rigid and stylized to a generous use of fabric, colours and abstract designs. Many Chasubles are decorated with an embroidered Y–shaped strip which is called the Orphrey and is a relic of the Pallium which is no longer worn, and now replaced by the stole.

Cope and Morse
The outer garment used as a cloak is worn on special occasions and in procession. Again the fabric and embroidery offer an opportunity for the designer and embroiderer to show their skills.

The Cope is virtually a semi-circle. The two edges of the front opening are usually edged with a broad band of embroidery called an Orphrey. The Hood has lost its original use and now hangs more as a decoration than for use. In some cases it is dispensed with altogether.

The Morse is the clasp which draws the two edges of the Cope together across the chest of the wearer. It can be quite elaborate, and some have jewels mounted on them.

Mitre
The Mitre is worn by Bishops in procession. It is virtually two triangles joined over the crown of the head. Two Lappets are attached at the back, and the whole folds flat. The embroidery usually goes around the base, i.e. a cross at the forehead and round the back of the head, rising to the front and back points.

Outer garments worn by the Priest's assistants

Dalmatic and Tunicle
These two vestments are similar, differing only in size and treatment. The tunicle is simpler, bearing a coloured Orphrey running from the neck to the hem back and front, whereas the Dalmatic is more elaborate and has a band running around the cuff and across the chest and the knees. Often these garments are thrown over the neck and tied down the sides.

Laundering
It would be a tragedy if, after you have made a set of linen, it should be spoilt by ignorance or sheer neglect. So here are some hints to pass on. All linen should be hand-washed in pure soap; not modern powders, which will contain bleach, blue dye and fluourescers for added 'brighter whiteness'. Several rinses in clean water will be necessary and the addition of Borax to the final rinse (one teaspoon to the gallon) will enhance the linen and slightly stiffen the fabric. Do *not* use starch.

Fold in a towel and leave for an hour. Iron on a deep pile with the embroidery face down, gently stretch to keep the correct shape and press – rather than iron – the embroidered part. The Fair Linen Cloth should be ironed until bone dry and rolled on a roller. The rest of the linen is folded and pressed as mentioned above. Surplices, Cottas, Albs and the Bishop's Rochet are all washed in a similar manner. The white Alb has nowadays been replaced by a white cassock and the Amice by a small hood or kerchief.

◀ **Fully robed Priest by the altar** Jeanette Morton

18
Metal thread work

Precious metals and jewels

Metal threads and precious jewels have been used in embroidery for thousands of years. Symbolism and myth were, and still are, attributes of these materials. One has only to consider the clothes and other adornments of courtly society and religious vestments, and literature has many allusions to their richness as a measure of status.

Underside couching

Today gold and silver threads are most familiar, and in their various forms these are couched to the background fabric. The most famous piece in England today is probably the Saint Cuthbert's Stole, *c.* AD 800, in Durham Cathedral. It is the remains of this Bishop's Stole and Maniple and was worked in underside couching. This is a method of laying the gold thread that is not practised today. The gold thread used was very fine, which enabled the linen thread to pull the gold through the linen fabric. This helped to preserve the linen thread and made the laid gold very supple. Only the gold is visible on the surface, giving an evenly-spaced, dimpled effect. Nowadays the metal threads used are constructed differently and have lost their suppleness; only two threads, called 'Passing' and 'Tambour', can be sewn through a suitable fabric.

Handling metal threads

When handling these threads it is important to keep them firmly twisted to avoid the core of silk showing through while the couching thread – of Maltese Silk called 'Mare's Tail' – is evenly spaced over two threads of gold to outline the design. Where the gold is laid close together, the overall effect is as though the fabric is in fact a cloth of gold. By using a contrasting thread and varying the couching

thread stitches from close to wide, the pattern of the design appears and this form of gold work is called 'Or Nué' – see chapter 17.

All this applies equally to silver threads, but as silver tarnishes, this material is not used very much. Silver and gold can be imitated in 'Lurex', which does not tarnish, but tends to be rather garish and the gold variety does not have the subtle lustre of real gold's reddish tinge.

Mounting jewels

In 1987 an exhibition of Russian court costumes was held at the Barbican Centre in London. A number of gowns were encrusted in gold or silver with headdresses to match. These must have been very heavy and uncomfortable to wear. The mounting of the jewels was treated in the same way as Indian embroidery treated Shisa Glass (mica). A strong thread was stitched across the jewel, perhaps several times, according to the size of the jewel. These threads were then buttonhole stitched together, which brought them down tightly to the base, thereby holding the jewel firmly. Pearls were pierced and attached by passing the thread through them like beads. Sequins were held in place with a bead or using 'Mare's Tail' couched through the centre hole. You should refer to Gay Swift's *Encyclopaedia of Embroidery Techniques* (Batsford) under 'Shisha' for excellent diagrams.

Many of these points are mentioned elsewhere in the text, especially in chapters 17 and 20.

Varieties of gold thread

Here is a short list of the main kinds of gold thread you will need to know about at this stage. Note that the gold thread known as 'Japanese' or 'Chinese' is made in several

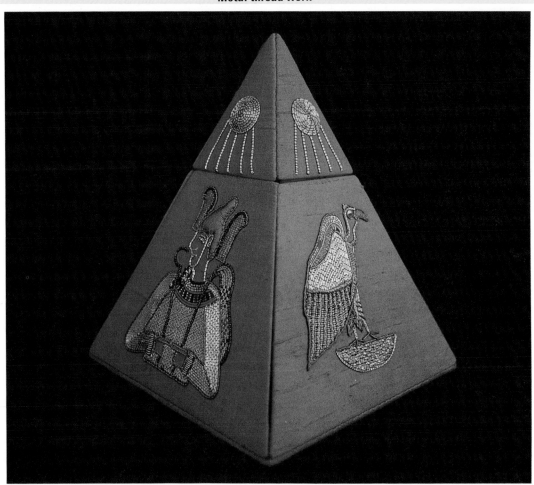

Egyptian box – closed Lorna Rand

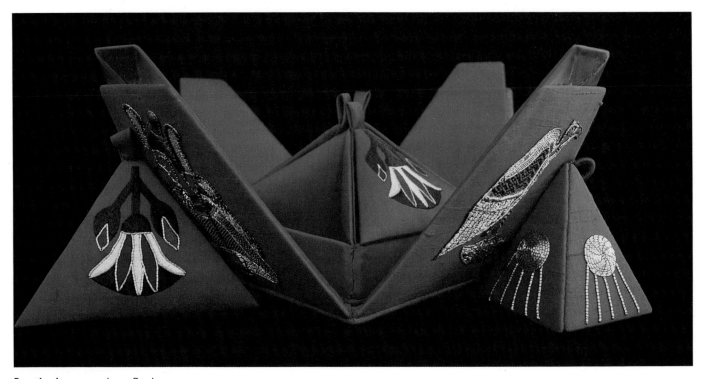

Egyptian box – open Lorna Rand

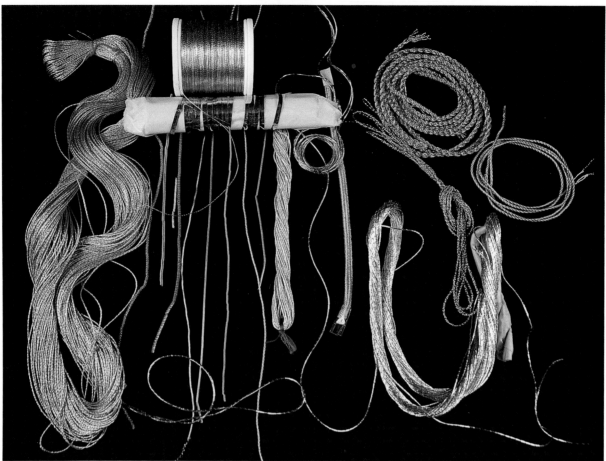

Metal thread in the studio

thicknesses by extruding the metal, beating it flat on paper, cutting this into strips, then winding it around a silk cord. Purl threads are made with wire with no silk core and are attached to the embroidery by cutting into small lengths and treating them as if they were beads – or, in the case of 'Pearl purl', by couching.

Cord	similar to above, but in many thicknesses
Crinkle	textured thread for added interest
Gimp	a decorated thread
Japanese gold thread	wrapped thread (also in silver and copper)
Passing thread	smooth and fine enough to pass through fabric
Plate	flat plate for crimping over a screw
Purl gold	
Check purl	mottled, sparkling, chequered finish
Large pearl purl	uses a springier wire
Pearl purl	heavier drawn, wire, not coiled too closely
Rough purl	muted, soft finish
Small check purl	uses a fine wire with mottled finish
Smooth purl	tightly coiled, highly polished drawn wire
Russia braid	like two cords needlewoven together
Soutâche	a smooth flat plaited thread
Tambour	very fine thread for sewing through a fabric
Twist	between a fine cord and a twisted ply
Wavy passing	similar to 'Passing' – less smooth and often finer

You should refer to Barbara Dawson *Metal Thread Embroidery* (see Bibliography).

19
Stumpwork

History

This form of embroidery flourished mostly in England during the seventeenth and eighteenth centuries. It seems to be a culmination of all the techniques learnt earlier by young women to demonstrate their prowess.

The work is sometimes three-dimensional and raised to give a life-like appearance to the figures, plants and animals which appear in the designs. It is also known as 'embroidery on the stump'. The boxes, mirrors and bags that have survived all show an inventiveness, albeit a trifle naïve, as the embroiderer strove to fill the surface first with a scene, probably taken from the Bible, with the characters dressed in Tudor or Stuart contemporary style, then with a castle or house surrounded by trees, plants and animals the size of which have no reference to scale.

The designs were collected from pattern books or illustrated books on plants or animals and used, quite literally, to fill in the spaces left in the main design. The leopard and the unicorn are always present. This form of embroidery was also practised on the Continent, particularly in Germany and, where some pieces remain, they have a heavily Gothic appearance.

Needle-made lace and detached buttonhole were widely used and the 'stumps' – that is, the raised work – were padded with a piece of leather or wood or simply stuffed to give the desired shape. These were then covered with wool and even hair in varying directions until the stump was entirely worked over in hatching. Detached chain stitch formed the loose pieces such as a flowing cloak, a skirt, a tent flap, a petal or a leaf.

Various intricate stitches were used to depict the limbs, which were sometimes articulated so that they could be moved, and so delicate that features of face and minute detail required much ingenuity.

It is an extraordinary form of embroidery which must have been time-consuming fun, while employing many jewels, silks, metallic threads, mica – for the windows – cord, gimp and plate. Many threads and fabrics seem to have been used, but the foundation was usually a cream silk laid over a backing of fine linen.

In the Student Room of the Victoria and Albert Museum in London, there are pieces of partially-finished work, Here you can see the designs and methods of work. Designs were sometimes drawn by a journeyman artist engaged on some other work at the house.

Method

Stretch a piece of fine calico or linen over your frame as a backing, then add a piece of silk fabric. There are, of course, other modern fabrics which could be used today. Draw out the area to be covered, for example the shape of a mirror frame, a box top or some other article. Then transfer your design, having first made the design to scale and considered the content.

Now comes the raised or padded work that will give realism to the tiny figures and other details. Sometimes the figure should be made separately on a piece of stiff paper or on a firm surface such as buckram, and then transferred to the fabric. The covering of the figure is most easily accomplished with buttonhole or lace stitch because they are flexible, and can be stretched over the padding and appliquéd to the fabric.

Because today we might not use leather or wood, another form of raising the stump is to cut a series of shapes, for example an arm, a leg or a jewel, in felt. Each shape is cut a little smaller. The largest shape is the final one. These are carefully appliquéd one over the other, beginning with the smallest, until the required depth is achieved. This shape is then covered with stitchery. Such details as hands may be formed with fine wire that has been bound with a suitable thread.

Needleweaving is another techniqe that forms a detached area. Wrapping card can prove useful in a modern design. After all, embroidery is never stagnant but moves forwards as fresh fabrics, threads and techniques are applied. Baskets were also made entirely in bead work with ribbon for decoration. These were sometimes quite large, about 30 cm (12 in) square. Lids of boxes often used the same technique with free-standing fruits and flowers.

Materials

Calico for the foundation, felts for the raised 'stumps', silk, or your other chosen fabric, for the decorative surface. Threads used would include silk, cotton, hair. Jewels, sequins and mica would also be included.

Wrinkles

As the most famous pieces of stumpwork are to be seen in the Victoria and Albert Museum, a visit is really essential if you are to be able to appreciate the uses to which this form of embroidery was put.

The embroidery also appears on the lavish clothes of the Tudor and Stuart periods. Mostly, we do not work so finely, but much fun can be had by inventing your own use for the techniques and by studying raised work in general. A cabinet maker might make you a box with working drawers. You could then cover this in the traditional manner.

20
Heraldic embroidery

Heraldry appears in many and diverse places on monuments, seals, insignia, stained glass windows and furniture, and is carved on stalls and bosses in cathedrals and churches. It is used when a person is ennobled and is also used in civic and national regalia and flags.

The right to use a coat of arms is granted to a person or body and its use is rigorously protected. This very brief description will enable the embroiderer to understand what it is that is being worked and also to realize the importance of getting every detail correct. You should research your subject and have the design checked by the right authority, either the owner of the Grant or the College of Heralds in London.

The use of Heraldry

To understand the use of heraldry we need to turn back to the Middle Ages when heraldry was an important means of identification both on the field of battle and at the jousting tournament. That is why it is so necessary, even today, to be exact about its use. It will, therefore, be helpful to know how to 'read' a coat of arms, as this will give you an insight into the language and symbols used. Readers will find *Boutell's Heraldry* essential for an authoritative treatment of the subject and Jacqueline Fearn's book *Discovering Heraldry* very useful for general study.

To help you to practise what you have learnt *The Siege of Caerlaverock* ed: C. W. Scott-Giles (Fitzalan Pursuivant Extraordinary) is fun, inexpensive and very useful for learning the terminology (see Bibliography).

Heraldic costume

Knights wore, over their armour, a Surcoat to protect them from the heat of the sun and from the damp of the atmosphere. In the thirteenth century the fashion of displaying arms on these Surcoats began and about 1325 the Surcoat altered shape and hung to the knees at the back and above the knees in front. This garment was called the Cyclas and it, in turn, was altered by shortening it at the back, when it became known as the Jupon.

By about 1360 the Jupon was a more close-fitting tunic, sometimes made of leather but also of silk. By the end of the fifteenth century, this garment, the forerunner of the Tabard, was no longer in use. The Tabard hung below the waist to the thighs, the sleeves were broad and came to the elbow with the sides left open.

A familiar example of the Tabard is that of the Black Prince preserved in Canterbury Cathedral. The original has been removed and a replica hangs in its place. This was the heraldic habit on which the arms of the wearer were embroidered.

The knights' horses also wore armour, called Trappers or Caparisons, and wealthy knights had their Trappers engraved with their arms. Trappers or Caparisons were also made from cloth on which the arms of the rider were embroidered. If you can visualize the colourful heraldry at the Field of the Cloth of Gold (1517), you will have some idea of heraldic display at that time.

Finally, the use of armour went out of fashion in the sixteenth century; but the Tabard remains in use today as the 'habit' of the heralds, and is also the name for the cloth which hangs from the silver trumpets of the State Trumpeters.

There was another garment which evolved from the Mantleing (also called Lambrequin) that hung from the helmet. In illustrations we see the formalized interpretation in the flowing fabric, which often looks more like acanthus leaves, and which is held in place by a wreath around the helmet and surmounted by the Crest.

Other items using heraldic embroidery

Women are also entitled to bear arms and these were often shown on their Côte-Hardie as illustrated in the Luttrell Psalter (1340). See: Barbara Snook, 'English Embroidery', in the Bibliography.

Except on the ceremonial occasions of Royal Weddings, the State Opening of Parliament or a military parade such as Trooping the Colour of a Regiment, it is unlikely that any display of heraldry would occur today, although military colours, some uniforms and saddle cloths are still embroidered.

Heraldic embroidery is also found on cushions, purses, seal bags, book bindings and table carpets (on linen in tent stitch) from when the comfort of houses improved and furniture began to be upholstered. Some examples remain in private houses and museums. This work would have been carried out by the women of the house. See: Lugg and Willcocks, *Heraldry for Embroiderers* in the Bibliography.

Opus Anglicanum

Ecclesiastical embroidery was always richly executed to the glory of God. Princes of the Church and nobles across the European Continent made gifts of copes and other vestments to other nobles and eccelesiastics. Many of these were made in England where the art of embroidery flourished during the twelfth and thirteenth centuries. This work is still referred to as *Opus Anglicanum* (translated: 'English Work') and you should refer to chapter 18 for more detail. Several pieces have survived despite their frail nature.

The population was severely reduced by the Black Death after which the work never reached the same standard of excellence, and though embroidery revived under Henry VIII and Elizabeth I it was, in comparison, rather clumsy. The workshops where men and women were rigorously controlled by the Guilds carried out most of this work, which was also done in the monasteries and convents.

The Syon Cope

A good example of *Opus Anglicanum* and the use of heraldry in embroidery is the Syon Cope, which may still be seen in the Victoria and Albert Museum, London, and appears in many of the books on the subject (see Bibliography).

The Cope was originally a Chasuble to which a circumferential Orphrey has been attached. This Orphrey is made from a stole and maniple, probably from the same set of eucharistic vestments. The design is of armorial lozenges set in squares of alternate red and green; the Morse is made up of three bands of similar heraldic squares. The heraldic embroidery is worked in silver-gilt thread and coloured silks in underside couching, cross stitch and plait stitch on linen.

The whole background is covered in a chevron pattern of split stitch. The overall design of the Cope is interlaced quatrefoils, the spaces between which have winged angels standing on wheels. The front Orphrey is again squares with lozenges filled with swans, peacocks and crosses. It is well worth a closer study for the treatment of the armorial lozenges. (See also chapter 17 and refer in the Bibliography to *English Mediaeval Embroidery* by Mrs Archibald Christie.)

Stitches and materials used

Stitches used are split stitch, cross stitch and plait stitch on linen, and underside couching for the metal threads.

Threads used are commonly a coloured floss silk, and various gold and silver-gilt metal threads with linen for the underside couching. Surface couching is also used but is not so long-lasting.

Embroidering on velvet

Two layers of linen are used when embroidering velvet, as the velvet plush surface is slippery. The design is drawn on the fine linen and worked through this on the coarser linen at the back of it. The work is then carefully cut away and applied to the velvet. If the garment is to be made in silk the design would be worked directly on the fabric. The Butler-Bowden Cope, which is also on display at the Victoria and Albert Museum in London, has examples of embroidery on velvet.

21

Some recent public embroideries by British embroiderers

Title and designer	Location
The Overlord Embroidery *Sandra Lawrence*	The D-day Museum, Portsmouth
The New Forest Embroidery *Belinda, Lady Montague*	Verderer's Court, Queen's House, Lyndhurst, Hants
The Chester Embroidery *Diana Springall*	The Town Hall, Chester
The Women's Institute Embroidery *Constance Howard*	Denman College, Marsham, Oxfordshire
The Quaker Tapestries *The Quaker Tapestry Group*	The Society of Friends, Friends' House, Euston, London
The Hastings Tapestry *Royal School of Needlework*	The Tridome, Hastings, Sussex
The Croydon Town Hall Embroidery *Moyra McNeill*	The Town Hall, Croydon, Surrey
1000 Years of the Monarchy *Audrey Walker*	The Pump Room, Bath
The Maidenhead Charter Hanging *Jan Beaney and Jean Littlejohn*	Maidenhead, Berkshire
The Exeter Rondels *Marjorie Dyer*	Exeter Cathedral, Exeter, Devon
The Spirit of Winchester Panel *Jean Baker*	Royal Hampshire County Hospital, Winchester
Panel for the Paragon Group Offices *Verina Warren*	Tampa, Florida, USA
The Cardross Church Panels *Hannah Frew-Patterson*	Cardross, Scotland

22

International embroidery

Should you be fortunate in working with a group of students, an effective way to learn is to divide the world into areas and for each member of the group to make a detailed study of the embroidery of one area, sharing the results with the others, but if you are working on your own, then rather more work will be needed.

This chapter is intended to draw to your attention some of the 'migrations' of embroidery. The many stitches and techniques embroiderers use are interrelated and you will find these relationships a rewarding study in themselves.

You should aim to know at least one foreign embroidery tradition well, with special attention to technique, use of regional materials and dyestuffs, symbolism, uses to which the finished articles would be put, the history of the origin and development of the tradition, and social pressures that may have caused it to develop as a distinct form.

For example, if you are studying Latin American embroidery, you will want to know a little about the interplay of the Aztec and the Spanish traditions, as well as the influence of more modern materials. You will also need to visit museums and galleries to see the embroidery in its original form and to relate it to other symbols in the society.

The Bibliography will introduce you to a wide selection of books on the subject and you may find that *An Illustrated History of Needlework* by Bridgeman and Drury is a particularly useful introduction.

Much European embroidery has been absorbed into the canon of British embroidery. This is particularly true with whitework, where Hedebo and Hardanger were brought to Scotland and became the foundation for Ayrshire work.

France and Italy offered Richelieu and Reticella – the latter classed as a kind of lace – and we have cutwork.

Greek lace, which uses the same withdrawn thread techniques as Richelieu, was brought to the English Lake District by the great Victorian John Ruskin and was taught as Ruskin work to relieve poverty in the area.

The Quakers took Jacobean stitches to the linen manufacturing area of southern Ireland around the town of Mountmellick to relieve poverty there. In the late nineteenth century this work became well-known and was extensively used in domestic whitework.

The Quakers also gave emigrants their patchwork 'kits', which travelled to Australia and the Americas, and some of these patchworks have now returned to England, for example log cabin from Canada. Blocks of patches joined together, sometimes with appliqué added, have come to us as American quilts with quite specific named designs such as Bear's Paw and Wedding Ring.

The distinctive cut-away appliqué of the San Blas Indians of Panama (Kuna) has joined the British repertoire as San Blas, while the Seminole Indians in Florida have adapted patchwork by sewing strips together and cutting them up diagonally to sew into new arrangements.

Rescht work is a kind of reverse appliqué (découpé) made in the eighteenth and early nineteenth centuries in and around the town of Rescht on the Caspian Sea.

More recently the Australians have used checked gingham worked in an embellished cross stitch which is called lacey cross stitch.

23
Embroidery conservation

Always be prepared to leave well alone. Many tragedies occur because of lack of knowledge; however, there are some really useful things that can be done with caution.

The hazards

Light, dirt, damp and atmosphere are the great enemies, so tackle these first: don't place the article in a strong light, as light fades and rots fabric. Don't keep it in a damp unventilated space as atmosphere, dampness and stagnant air set up moulds which eat away at fabric.

Of course we want to see older embroideries, to enjoy them, so display them in a north-facing light, and handle them very carefully, preferably with thin cotton or polythene gloves. Keep the article as clean as possible – dirt includes of small grains of dust which rub away at the threads. Never fold articles away in a polythene or other non-breathing wrapping; use acid-free tissue paper.

Surface dust should be removed gently. Using a vacuum cleaner with the nozzle firmly covered with gauze and held not too near the article will remove surface dust, as the accumulation of the dirt on the gauze soon proves. A small piece of fresh white bread may be used as a cleaning pad and gently rolled across a stain, but very gentle use is necessary, lest you inadvertently rub away the thread as well.

Perspiration from the body will eventually rot fabrics; the underarm areas of silk clothes are especially vulnerable to this decay.

Atmosphere is something we can improve. A damp, unaired room or wall cupboard are preventable situations. When storing articles, a dust cover helps. Acid-free tissue paper should be laid between articles and used when they are rolled up. Always roll with the surface facing the outside, over a covered cardboard roll. The cupboard, drawer, or shelf needs to be in a properly ventilated position free from moths or other insects.

Washing

A few, but not very many, embroidered articles can be washed; test for fibre and colour fastness first (the latter may be done with slightly moistened blotting paper gently pressed on a small area of the underside).

Wash such articles as can be washed. Avoid cheap detergents and washing powders, as many of these contain bleach and fluourescers to make articles 'whiter than white.' You should especially avoid 'biological' powders, which can eat away protein fibres such as wool. Linen and cotton should be washed in pure soap flakes and well rinsed. Some articles, particularly lace, can be placed in a jar of this solution and gently shaken. Carefully spread the fabric out to dry on a clean white towel or, in the case of lace, wind around a jar and carefully stretch into shape.

'Lissapol' is a pure detergent: use a one per cent solution obtained by adding 10 ml to one litre of distilled water.

Saponaria Officinalis is a plant which used to be used as a soap. If you have bought it as a prepared extract, use according to the instructions on the packet. Make a small quantity, as it does not keep. Otherwise, make a solution with *Saponaria Officinalis* twigs and distilled water. In the absence of distilled water (easily obtained from pharmacists) use rainwater that has been filtered several times through an activated carbon or *clean* coffee filter to remove sediment and use it cool for washing. Always rinse all embroideries at least three times in distilled water. Remember that acid rain is a new hazard.

In no case should any article be rubbed. It is

St Mary's Church Netherbury, frontal cross – before restoration

St Mary's Church Netherbury, frontal cross – after restoration

far better to repeat the operation several times very gently than to indulge in tremendous washday fervour. A sponge may be pressed gently and systematically across the article, which should first be placed flat without folds in a shallow plastic or glass container. Use a polythene sheet to make a large 'pond' for large articles. All these operations need time and a gentle touch. It is often the human hand that has caused the wear in the first place.

Dry cleaning

This should be done only with great caution. Certainly you should not place any embroidery into the drum of the local coin-operated machine at the cleaners. Go to a specialist cleaner and be prepared to sew the item into a white cotton bag to avoid it snagging. You may have to sign a disclaimer for damage before the cleaner will attempt to do it at all.

Restoration

This is very time-consuming and expensive and can only be used in some instances. Embroideries often last longer than the fabric on which they are worked. It is possible to lift them intact and transfer them to a suitable new fabric by using an appliqué method. It is possible to couch down threads that have come loose, and a worn area can, if you have threads that match in texture and colour, be, as it were, 're-embroidered'. Many articles must, regretfully, be taken out of use. A carefully applied fine net will hold some articles together for display only.

Caution: these suggestions have all been practised with success, but the need for caution must be stressed; when in doubt, you should seek help from an expert.

Seek advice

The Victoria and Albert Museum, London will give advice free of charge. They publish leaflets and technical notes on the care of textiles. The Textile Conservation Centre at Hampton Court, Molesey, Surrey, England will also give excellent advice. Consult *Care and Preservation of Textiles* by Karen Finch and G. Putnam (see Bibliography).

24
Recording your embroidery

Introduction

This chapter offers a short introduction to photographing your embroidery for the record – not to photography as a subject in itself. It covers some technical ground and you should approach it with the same relaxed sense of purpose as other chapters on stitches and embroidery techniques. Just as you learn to compose an embroidery and to carry it out with technical accomplishment, so here you will need to concentrate on the possibilities of the camera lens and its effect on the film.

There are two main themes: one is to ensure that the embroidery is set up so that the lens can see what you want to photograph – and nothing else. The second is to ensure that the camera will record the image faithfully as you want it, and not as circumstances have, perhaps unfortunately, dictated.

All is not quite what it seems in the camera's world: light has colour; lenses can distort shape and colour, and hide what they are looking at; softness is a function of light and shadow and not of texture; sharp focus can depend on the speed of your film.

The camera body

A 35 mm format (or larger) Single Lens Reflex (SLR) camera is essential so that you can see 'through the single lens' exactly what you will see on the photograph. Additionally, the light meter will usually measure the light entering through the lens, which is a very great convenience.

Results are likely to be disappointing with cameras that use disc films or 10 mm format ('110' or 'tripper') cameras. The film format for these is very small and the lenses used are seldom appropriate for work of this kind.

Automation

While automation is very useful in some parts of the camera, it can prove to be a major handicap on occasions when you want to override the camera's calculations. You should avoid cameras with:

1. A permanent automatic flash gun. This is are not necessary and will ensure that photographs of your work are disappointing.
2. Permanent automatic focus – this might be a great boon in action photography, but is a liability when trying to compose an accurately focused shot of rather small, sometimes indistinct, and hairy features.
3. Permanent automatic exposure where you are unable to set an override for the aperture opening. Remember that you may want to expose the shot three times with 'bracketed' exposure, i.e. with 'over' exposure, then 'correct' exposure and finally with 'under' exposure.

If you are inexperienced, try to find an ordinary 35 mm SLR camera with a flexible automatic exposure control. This permits you to set the aperture as an override value ('aperture priority'), offers a means of bracketing the exposure – preferably other than by altering the aperture setting – and will have a proper set of focusing aids built into the viewfinder, such as a pair of semi-circular prisms. A 'stop-down' facility on the lens is very useful.

Visit reputable second-hand photographic equipment stores, but do check that service and parts are still available for the camera you are offered. This is especially true for the more automated electronic models.

Viewfinders

Cameras which have a separate viewfinder lens do not allow a sufficiently accurate view

Seed time – a subject for embroidery

of the area that will be included in the picture. Worse, by viewing from a slightly different angle, they may show a rather different interplay of light and object from that which the lens will 'see'.

Lenses
Focal length
The 'standard' 50 mm focal length lens comes

closest to approximating the human eye. Any lens with a longer focal length (e.g. 100 mm) may be referred to as a telephoto lens, and any shorter focal length (e.g. 35 mm) as a wide-angle lens. Wide-angle lenses are generally able to focus better on objects closer to the lens, and can often be reversed on the camera body mount to work in close-up.

The most useful lens for recording your

work is the relatively modest 35 mm or 28 mm wide-angle lens. So-called 'zoom' lenses are available with focal lengths between say, 28 mm and 75 mm, but these may give you lower image quality than a fixed lens because of their complexity.

Aperture

The aperture of a lens, for present purposes, is the amount that the lens iris will open to let light into the camera. It is quoted in 'f. numbers' and the maximum opening (say, f. 2) is quoted in lens catalogues. Usually a lens will close down to f. 22 as the smallest opening.

The smaller the opening, the deeper the space beyond the camera lens that is in sharp focus will be. This is called the 'depth of field', and with a small aperture setting you will find focus easier. (Note, however, the possible penalty that you will need a longer exposure time or a faster film.) Wide-angle lenses usually have larger maximum apertures, and telephoto lenses smaller ones, so that wide-angle lenses are easier to focus and can work faster in low light levels.

Focus and perspective – 'stopping down'

Remember to focus on the most important part of the picture. Use all the focusing aids that your camera offers, but only use auto-focus with caution. A lens which you can 'stop-down' (closing down the aperture to a chosen value while previewing the shot) to check the depth of field visually is a boon. If you elect to use a small aperture to create greater depth of field, remember that you will need to focus on the centre of that area.

A long focal length (telephoto) lens will bring objects closer while foreshortening perspective. This effect is seen in photographs of motorway traffic which you know to be well spaced-out and travelling fast, yet looks as though it is stuck in a traffic jam.

Any lens with a shorter focal length (wide-angle) will enhance the perspective effect; a good example of this perspective is someone sitting on a park bench photographed at an angle, showing the bench as stretching far away.

Close-up work

To obtain a more close-up or 'magnified' picture you can use bellows, extension tubes (both move the lens away from the camera body) or magnifying filters (which act like a magnifying glass). 'Macro' lenses are specifically designed to permit close-up, detailed pictures. All can be useful (if sometimes expensive) options for photographing small areas of stitches. Telephoto lenses are inappropriate.

The less expensive magnifying filters can introduce some extra distortion, fuzziness of focus or colour peculiarities into your picture. No more than two should be used together. You may prefer to experiment using a lens reversing adapter and your wide-angle lens mounted the opposite way to normal on the camera to approach the same effect. If your camera permits this, it may be the least expensive option and prove flexible; reversing adapters are available for most SLR cameras and are not costly.

If you work in close-up, focusing is sometimes awkward. Note especially that, when using a reversing adapter and looking down at the subject, you will have to focus using the tripod height control – more difficult to steel yourself to try than actually to do – and you will also want to 'stop down' the aperture to give yourself the sharpest focus.

Lighting

The colour of light

All light has some colour cast although one may assume that the light from the open sky without direct sunlight in the middle of a fine day, is reasonably neutral. Daylight temperature is the normal colour balance for films.

Diffused light

Direct daytime sunshine, except possibly in a northern winter, is too bright for accurate rendering of subtle colour, which requires the softer light and shadow created by indirect light. To diffuse light, you can try several methods: the first is simply to put a diffuser over the light source (for example, taping greaseproof paper over windows); and the second is to reflect the light off something.

A plain white bedsheet makes a good reflector of light. A reflective 'Space Blanket' – easily obtained from sports shops and suitably scrunched up to prevent highlights – is more effective still, but you need to remember that while it will reflect a lot of light, that light is going to be rather hard. A white bedsheet or a large sheet of white card that reflects less, but softer, light will usually prove to be at least as effective. Should you find a 'space blanket' with a gold surface avoid it, as the colour cast from it will be extremely powerful.

Adding light
For main light, use daylight and avoid using flashguns. In the hands of an expert, these are useful and sometimes indispensable. For the beginner, however, they can be a major waste of costly film. Remember you will get discolouration if you bounce flash or any other light off even pale-coloured surfaces.

Photoflood bulbs are appropriate for main lighting, especially if used with a white 'umbrella' reflector, but they are expensive, have only a short life, and may require a special holder. If there is insufficient daylight to achieve a reasonably fast exposure, use several of the now freely available 'daylight-matching' bulbs as fill-in; these can be mounted in an 'Anglepoise' light or small spotlight.

Background fill lights are low-powered lights used to fill in the shadow side of a piece where a plain white card reflector is too weak to do the same job. Detail emphasis lights are used with larger pieces to emphasize areas of interest.

Shade and lighting angles
As light falls on an object it produces highlights and shadows where the surface alters and undulates. Within reason, the softer the light (the lower the absolute light level and the more diffuse), the more it is possible to show up the surface modelling and to bring out the most subtle colour. The beginner will need to experiment with this for some time before it becomes an instinct. It is in this area – training the eye to observe the interplay of light and shadow – rather than in the purchase of glamorous equipment that the beginner will find the most rewarding results.

Films
Transparencies will provide better definition and colour than prints.

Film speed and sensitivity
To avoid excessively 'grainy' photographs you should limit your film speed to 200 ASA. Set an absolute maximum of 400 ASA. For the very best results, you may choose to keep the film speed down to 25 ASA, and learn to use lighting and slower exposures. In general you will want to avoid any exposure slower than about one and a half seconds. Very slow exposures can result in so-called ('reciprocity failure' when doubling the exposure time or opening up the lens aperture by one stop gives you no longer double, but perhaps only one third, greater exposure.

Film colour balance and filters
Films are balanced for particular lighting conditions. Normally you will be sold a film balanced for daylight, but you should be aware that you can also purchase films balanced to avoid the excessive yellow cast of tungsten lighting. Ordinary fluorescent light should be avoided; it usually has a marked colour cast which will affect the quality of your pictures. It is wise to use standard daylight films and avoid messing about with filters and tungsten balanced films.

Tripods and steadiness
Tripods are essential as they offer the chance to check the composition of the photo carefully and to make alterations easily. For best results you should use a remote shutter trigger and a time delay on the camera to avoid all movement. Tripods should be well-made, solid and have a wide range of adjustment. The head needs to tilt and swivel, but a worm drive mechanism for height is not necessary.

Should you need to take a photograph without a tripod, you will need to steady the camera. Use a bean bag to rest the camera on, plus a remote shutter trigger.

Backgrounds and colour

The colour of the walls, the furnishings, and the floor of the room you use will reflect light on to the subject you wish to photograph. It is important to notice where you may pick up a stray colour cast and be ready with white sheets that can be laid over that favourite bright green rug, brown sofa, red lacquer cabinet, pale peach curtains or beneath the expensively redecorated Wedgewood green ceiling.

Background materials

Use soft, easily draped material with neutral tones, black velvet to hide all background or long wide rolls of neutral-coloured paper to help to give a featureless background. Avoid patterns and strong colours at all costs.

Props

Use cushions, bean bags, bookends and so on as supports under the draped background material. Set these up remembering that the embroidery is the thing you want to record, not an artfully contrived studio set-up. Provided it is out of sight, steady and does not affect the colour, you can use anything to get the effect you want.

Using your eyes

Stray detail

Develop the habit of looking all round the eyepiece to spot all those stray threads, hairs, bits of fluff, pieces of obtruding background furniture, light switches, and other gremlins. Seeing what is actually there is one of the trickiest parts of photography. Pick up fluff with a strip of masking tape wound around your hand tacky side out.

Lens flare

This is an occasional problem when direct light from a bright source enters the lens.

Watch for it from very reflective surfaces in your embroidery and change the light source position, or use a lens hood to shade the lens from lights shining sideways on.

Centering the photograph

Make quite sure that the camera body is properly centred on the embroidery so that it is correctly opposite the piece, square to the lens.

Surface detail

Train yourself to look at the embroidery through the lens and to see it in the two dimensions of the photograph, rather than the three dimensions of the embroidery. Surface detail matters: if you have some feature on the surface of the embroidery that you want to highlight, you may have to alter the angle of the camera lens so that it shows up against the backdrop rather than hiding in front of a similar-coloured part of the embroidery itself.

Photographing through glass

You will want to avoid stray reflections should you be unable to remove the piece from its frame. Quite a good method is to set it up so that the frame is facing slightly downwards from vertical at a piece of black velvet; the camera is then set low on the tripod so that it looks upwards squarely at the face of the frame. Sometimes use of a 'Polaroid' filter may help.

Using your other senses

Listen to make sure no lorries or trains are rumbling by outside. Avoid draughty situations where a breeze may move the threads on the piece, and people walking across wooden floors or closing doors, which may set up vibrations. Remember too that distracting sights and sounds are a menace. If you are trying to concentrate it is helpful to find occupations elsewhere for spouses, children and pets and to turn off the TV.

Bibliography

Arranged in alphabetical order by subject,
and then by title

This is, necessarily, a very selective bibliography. Students will wish to explore the individual bibliographies in these books for detailed lists on each subject. You should expect to use all the resources available to you – including your local public and reference libraries, nearby art college, polytechnic and university libraries, as well as the libraries in museums, and specialist societies such as The Embroiderers' Guild, The Royal School of Needlework and the West Country Embroiderers, which are only open to members.

The latest edition or reprint has been cited where possible, but some titles run back for 80 years or more and have been republished by a series of publishers. If you have difficulty in obtaining a title, remember that it may be available under a different ISBN reference.

For foreign embroideries you may be able to seek help from Embassy Cultural Attachés.

Please note that:
DMC stands for
    Dollfus-Mieg & Cie S.A., Mulhouse, France,
HMSO stands for
    His/Her Majesty's Stationery Office, UK government publishers

Both DMC and Dover Publications offer a very complete range of design sources; seek them second-hand as well as new.

A list of major international museums and galleries can be found in P.Clabburn: *Needleworker's Dictionary*, and good bibliographies will be found in that book and in the other books listed here.

Appliqué

Appliqué   *E. Shearns & D. Fielding*   Pan 1974   0 330 23866 3
The Big Book of Appliqué   *Virginia Avery*   Bell & Hyman   1979   0 7135 1187 7
Creative Appliqué   *Beryl Dean*   Studio Vista   1970   0 289 79708 X
Needlecraft 1: Appliqué   *Joan Cleaver*   Search Press   1978   0 85532 408 2
Notes on Appliqué Work and Patchwork   *Victoria & Albert Museum*   HMSO   1947
Appliqué: A Practical Approach   *Dorothy Tucker*   Batsford   1989   0 7134 5349 4

Assisi

Assisi Embroidery   DMC Thread Co.
Assisi Embroidery   *Eva-Maria Leszner*   Batsford   1988   0 7134 5596 9
Assisi Embroidery: techniques and 42 charted designs   *Pamela Miller*   Ness   Constable/Dover   1979
    0 486 23743 5
Assisi Pattern Books 1–3   DMC Thread Co.

Basic stitches

Complete Encyclopedia of Needlework   *Thérèse de Dillmont*   DMC/Brackan Books   1987   1 85170 014 5
Constance Howard's Book of Stitches   *Constance Howard*   Batsford   1979   0 7134 1006 X
Creative Stitches   *Edith John*   Dover   1974   0 486 22972 6
Decorating with Stitches   *L. de Denne & M. Johnson*   Butler & Tanner   1975   0 7135 1932 0
English Embroidery   *A. E. Kendrick*   Batsford/Black   1910/1967
50 Freestyle Embroidery Stitches   *J & P Coats*

Mary Thomas' Dictionary of Embroidery Stitches   *Mary Thomas*   Hodder & Stoughton   1983
    0 340 34662 0
Samplers & Stitches   *Mrs Archibald (Grace) Christie*   Pitmans   1934

Bead Work

The Bead Embroidered Dress   *Joan Edwards*   Bayford   1986   0 907287 06 9

Bibliography

Batsford Encyclopedia of Embroidery Techniques   *Gay Swift*   Batsford   1984   0 7134 3932 7
Embroidery: a Reader's Guide   *Kathleen Mary Harris*   Cambridge University Press   1950
Needlework: a selected Bibliography   *Ed: Sestay*   Scarecrow   1983   0 8108 1554 0
Needleworker's Dictionary   *Pamela Clabburn*   Macmillan   1976   0 333 18756 3

Blackwork

Art of Blackwork Embroidery   *Rosemary Drysdale*   Mills & Boon   1975   0 263 05995 2
Blackwork   *Joan Edwards*   Bayford   1980   0 907 28700 X
Blackwork Embroidery   *Geddes & McNeill*   Dover   1976   0 486 23245 X
Blackwork Embroidery   *Margaret Pascoe*   Batsford   1989   0 7134 5146 7

Boxes and Constructions

Embroidered Boxes   *Jane Lemon*   Batsford   1984   0 7134 4587 4
Making Historical Costume Dolls   *J. Cassin-Scott*   Batsford   1987   0 7134 5765 1
Textile Sculpture   *Irene Waller*   Taplinger   1977   0 8008 7579 6

Canvas Work

Bargello: Florentine Canvas Work   *E. S. Williams*   Van Nostrand   1967   0 442 29481 6
Berlin Work   *Joan Edwards*   Bayford   1980   0 907 287 01 8
Canvas Work   *Jennifer Gray*   Batsford   1974   0 7134 4769 9
Canvas Work Embroidery   *Diana Springall*   Batsford   1969   0 7134 2602 0
Dictionary of Canvas Work Stitches   *Mary Rhodes*   Batsford   1989   0 7134 3302 7
Florentine Canvas Embroidery   *Barbara Snook*   Batsford   1967
Glorious Needlepoint   *Kaffe Fassett*   Century   1987   0 7126 1693 4
Ideas for Canvas Work   *Mary Rhodes*   Batsford   1984   0 7134 4613 7
Needlecrafts 2: Canvas Work   *Norah Jones*   Search Press   1978   0 85532 409 0
Needlepoint – The Art of Canvas Embroidery   *Mary Rhodes*   Octopus   1974   0 7064 0363 0
A Picture Book for Kneeler Makers   *Joan Edwards*   Bayford   1984   0 907287 05 0

Colour

Art School *Ed. C. Saxton* Chartwell/QED 1981   0 89009 521 3
Colour *Ed. H. Varley* Marshall/Leisure 1988   0 9507901 1
Colour for the Artist   *Schwarz*   Studio Vista   1980   0 289 70972 5
Designer's Guide to Colour Vols I, II, III   Angus & Robertson   1988
                                    Vol I   1984   0 207 15023 0
                                    Vol II   1985   0 207 15130 X
                                    Vol III   1986   0 207 15488 0
Embroidery and Colour   *Constance Howard*   Batsford   1986   0 7134 5419 9
Principles of Color   *Faber Birren*   Schiffer   1977   0 442 20774 3

Conservation

Care and Preservation of Textiles   *K. Finch & G. Putnam*   Batsford   1985
    0 7134 4411 8
Textiles – their care and preservation in Museums   *Glover*   Museums Association   1973
    0 902102 44 3

Design

And so to Embroider   *Needlework Development Scheme*   University of London Press   1960
Art Nouveau   *G. Warren*   Octopus   1974   0 86178 114 7
Creative Art of Embroidery   *Barbara Snook*   Hamlyn   1972   0 600 31752 8
Creative Drawing   *Rottger and Klaute*   Batsford   1976   0 7134 2353 6
Design and Form   *Johannes Itten*   Thames and Hudson   1975   0 500 27006 7 8
Design for Embroidery: a fine art approach   *Diana Springall*   Pelham Books   1984   0 7207 1755 8
Design for Embroidery from Traditional English Sources   *Constance Howard*   Batsford   1989
   0 7134 6299 X
Design in Embroidery   *Kathleen Whyte*   Batsford   1983   0 7134 4137 2
Design Sources for Embroidery   *Muriel Best & Vicky Lugg*   Batsford   1988   0 7134 5573 X
Design Sources for the Fibre Artist   *Irene Waller*   Davis Pubs.   1978   0 87192 098 0
Designing with String   *Mary Seyd*   Batsford   1967   0 7134 2260 2
Drawing and Design for Embroidery   *Richard Box*   Batsford   0 7134 5547 0
Embroiderer's Workbook   *Jan Messent*   Batsford   1988   0 7134 5709 0
Embroidery and Architecture   *Jan Messent*   Batsford   1985   0 7134 3703 0
Embroidery and Design on Patterned Fabric   *Anne Kenyon*   David and Charles   1975   0 7153 6189 9
Embroidery and Nature   *Jan Messent*   Batsford   1983   0 7134 1832 X
Embroidery Design   *Jan Messent*   Search Press   1979   0 85532 426 0
Embroidery Designs from the Sea   *Barbara Snook*   Dryad Press Ltd   1986   0 85219 682 2
Embroidery: Principles of Design   *Lilian Rogers*   Cambridge University Press   1980   0 521 21556 0
Enjoying Embroidery   *Anne Wilson*   Batsford   1975   0 7134 2984 4
Experimental Embroidery   *Edith John*   Batsford   1976   07134 3060 5
Faces and Figures in Embroidery   *V. Campbell-Harding*   Batsford   1985   0 7134 1099 X
Fertile Image   *Paul Nash (Ed: M. Nash)*   Faber   1975   0 571 10636 6
Inspiration for Embroidery   *Constance Howard*   Batsford   1985   0 7134 4768 0
Let's Start Designing   *Pat Scrase*   Studio Vista/Reinhold   1966
Magic Worlds of Fantasy   *Diana Douglas Duncan*   Harcourt Brace   1978   0 15 155102 2
Modern Design in Embroidery   *Rebecca Crompton*   Batsford   1936
Needlework, designs for miniature projects   *Folk*   Dover   1985   0 486 24660 4
Textiles by William Morris & Co 1861–1940   *O. Fairclough & E. Leary*   Thames and Hudson   1981
   0 500 27225 5
Textile Crafts   *Ed: Constance Howard*   Pitman/Scribners   1978   0 684 15507 9

Dyes and Dyeing

Batik   *Christian Albrecht*   Search Press   1974
Create your own Natural Dyes   *Kathleen Schultz*   Sterling   1975/82   0 8069 7576 8
Fabric Dying and Printing. 3: screen printing   *S. & P. Robinson*   Dryad Ltd   1976   0 85219 096 4
Fabric Printing   *Gisela Hein*   Batsford   1972   0 7134 2382 X
Manual of Dyes and Fabrics   *Joyce Storey*   Thames and Hudson   1978   0 500 68016 7
The Use of Vegetable Dyes   *Violetta Thurstan*   Dryad Press Ltd   1977   0 85219 094 8
Vegetable Dyes   *Ethel Mairet*   Faber   1952

Ecclesiastical Embroidery

Church Needlework   *Beryl Dean*   Batsford   1961   0 7134 6405 4
Church Needlework   *Hinda M. Hands*   Faith Press   1920
Church Needlework 1. Altar Linen   *Kathleen Harris*   Embroiderers' Guild   1959
Ecclesiastical Embroidery   *Beryl Dean*   Batsford   1989   0 7134 6252 3
Embroidery for Religion & Ceremonial   *Beryl Dean*   Batsford   1986   0 7134 5280 3
English Art 871–1100   *Prof. D. Talbot-Rice*   Oxford University Press   1952
English Embroidery   *A. F. Kendrick*   Batsford   1910
English Mediæval Embroidery   *Mrs Archibald (Grace) Christie*   Oxford   1938
Threads of Gold: The embroideries and textiles of York Minster   *Ed: Elizabeth Ingram*   Pitkin   1987   0
85372 427 X

Fabrics and Threads

The Essentials of Yarn Design for Handspinners   *Mabel Ross*   Mabel Ross–Kinloss   1983   0 9507292 1 3
Fabrics for Embroidery   *Jean Littlejohn*   Batsford   1986   0 7134 5112 2
Thread: An Art Form   *Irene Waller*   Studio Vista   1973   0 289 70224 0

Finishings

The Ashley Book of Knots   *Clifford W. Ashley*   Faber/Doubleday   1975   0 571 09659 X
Complete Encyclopaedia of Needlework   *Thérèse de Dillmont*   DMC/Brackan Books   1987   1 85170 0145
Creative Needlecraft   *Lynette de Denne*   Sundial Books   1979   0 904 23084 8

General reference

Art in Needlework   *Lewis F. Day & M. Buckle*   Batsford   1926
Batsford Encyclopaedia of Embroidery Techniques   *Gay Swift*   Batsford   1984   0 7134 3932 7
Complete Encyclopaedia of Needlework   *Thérèse de Dillmont*   DMC/Brackan   Books   1987   1 85170 0145
Creative Needlecraft   *Lynette de Denne*   Sundial Books   1979   0 904 23084 8
Dictionary of Needlework (1882 Facsimile)   *Caulfield & Saward*   Blaketon Hall   1989   0 907854 10 9
The Dictionary of Needlework   *Caulfield & Saward*   Dover/Constable   1972   2 vols:
   vol. 1   0 486 22800 2   vol. 2   0 486 22801 0
Mary Thomas' Dictionary of Stitches   *Mary Thomas*   Hodder   1983   0 340 34662 0
Mary Thomas' Embroidery Book   *Mary Thomas*   Hodder   1983   0 340 34663 9

Gold and metal thread work

Dictionary of Metal Thread Embroidery   *Jane Lemon*   Batsford   1987   0 7134 6516 6
Gold and Silver Embroidery   *Kit Pyman*   Search Press   1985   0 85532 588 7
Gold Work (Needlecrafts 20)   *Valerie Harding*   Search Press   1983   0 85532 455 4
Metal Thread Embroidery   *Barbara Dawson*   Batsford   1987   0 7134 5577 2

Hangings

1000 Years of Monarchy   *Audrey Walker*   The Assembly Rooms   Bath, Avon
The Bayeux Tapestry   *Queen Matilda*   Bayeux Tapestry Museum   Bayeux, Normandy, France
The Chester Hanging   *Diana Springall*   The City Hall, Chester   Chester City Council
The Hastings Embroidery   *Royal School of Needlework*   The Tridome, Hastings Borough Council
   Hastings, Sussex
The New Forest Embroidery   *Belinda Montagu*   Verderer's Hall, Lyndhurst, Hampshire
The New World Tapestry   Contact: *Tom Mor*,   77 Hyde Park Road, Plymouth, Devon PL3 4JN
The Overlord Embroidery   *Sandra Lawrence*   The D-Day Museum, Southsea   Portsmouth and
   Southsea City Council
The Quaker Tapestry   *Anne Wynn-Wilson*   A Description   0 9511 581 04
The Ribbon Book   *ed: Marianne Philbin*   Lark Books
The Women's Institute Hanging   *Federation of Women's Institutes*   Denman College, Buckinghamshire

Heraldic Embroidery

Boutell's Heraldry   *Revised: Scott-Giles, Brooke-Little*   Frederick Warne & Co.   1970
Discovering Heraldry   *Jacqueline Fearn*   Search Press   0 85263 476 5
English Heraldic Embroidery   *Clara Lamb*   Victoria & Albert Museum   1976
Heraldry for Embroidery   *Vicky Lugg & John Willcocks*   Batsford   1989   0 7134 6367 8
Heraldry in England   *Anthony Wagner*   Penguin   1946
Mediæval Heraldry   *Terence Wise*   Osprey   1980   0 85045 348 8
The Siege of Cærlaverock   *ed: C.W. Scott-Giles*   Heraldry Society, London   1979   0 904858 02 2

History of embroidery

20th Century Embroidery   *Constance Howard*   Batsford
   Vol 1: Great Britain to 1939   1981   0 7134 3942 4
   Vol 2: Great Britain 1940–1963   1983   0 7134 3944 0

Vol 3: Great Britain 1964–1977   1984   0 7134 4227 1
Vol 4: Great Britain from 1978   1986   0 7134 4658 7
Antique Needlework   *Lanto Synge*   Blandford Press   1989   0713 72128 6
The Art of Crewel Embroidery   *Mildred J. Davis*   Nelson/Crown/Vista   1963
Batsford Encyclopedia of Embroidery Techniques   *Gay Swift*   Batsford   1984   0 7134 3932 7
Chronicle of Embroidery 1900–1950   *Joan Edwards*   Bayford   1980   0 907287 02 6
Crewel Embroidery in England   *Joan Edwards*   Batsford/Morrow   1975   0 7134 3028 1
Designing for Embroidery from Ancient & Primitive Sources   *Jan Messent*   Studio Vista   1976
   0 289 70600 9
Discovering Embroidery of the 19th century   *Santina Levy*   Shire/Search Press   1971   0 85263 398 X
Dorothy Benson & the Embroidery Dept. of the Singer Sewing M/c Co.   *Joan Edwards*   Batsford   1988
   0 902287 07 7
Gertrude Jekyll   *Joan Edwards*   Bayford   1981   0 907287 03 4
History of English Embroidery   *Barbara Snook*   Bell & Hyman   1974   0 263 05579 5
Needlework Designs from the American Indians   *Anne C. Landsman*   Brunswick/Barnes   1977
Needlework of Mary Queen of Scots   *Margaret Swain*   Van Nostrand   1973
Needleworker's Dictionary   *Pamela Clabburn*   Macmillan   1976   0 333 18756 3
The Needle's Excellency   *Victoria & Albert Museum*   HMSO   1973   90 14 86 60 4
Old Patchwork Quilts and the women who made them   *Ruth E. Finley*   Branford/Bell   1929/1970

History of embroidery tools

A Guide for Collecting Needlework Tools   *Eleanor Johnson*   Shire Album 38   1978   0 85263 446 3
Illustrated History of Needlework Tools   *Gay Ann Rogers*   J. Murray   1983   0 7195 4021 6
Needlework Tools and Accessories   *Molly Proctor*   Batsford   1990   0 7134 5895 X
Old Needlework Boxes and Tools   *Mary Andere*   David and Charles   1971   0 7153 5260 1
Old Sewing Machines   *Carol Head*   Shire Press   1982   0 85263 591 5
Oldtime tools and toys of needlework   *Gertrude Whiting*   Dover   1972   0486 22517 8

International embroidery

American Needlework   *G. B. Harbeson*   Bonanza Books, N. Y.   1938
Ancient Civilisations Series
   (Small Books based on a series broadcast by the BBC and an excellent general introduction to the art of
   these regions)
   Covers: Egypt, Crete, India, China, Mexico and Peru   BBC Publications   1963
The Art of Judaic Needlework   *Ita Aber*   Bell & Hyman   1980   0 7135 1239 3
The Art of Oriental Embroidery   *Young Yang Chung*   Bell & Hyman   1980   0 7135 1205 9
Blue and White – the Cotton Embroideries of Rural China   *M. Baker & M. Lunt*   Sidgewick & Jackson
   1978   0 283 98481 3
Chinese Court Costume   Royal Scottish Museum   1980
Chinese Court Robes   *Edmund Capon/Victoria & Albert Museum*   HMSO
Chinese Folk Designs, a collection of 300 cut paper designs   *W M Hawley*   Dover   1972   0 486 22633 6
Chinese Folk Embroidery   *Yareng*   Thames and Hudson   1987   0 500 27463 0
Chinese Painting and the Decorative Style   *Ed. M. Medley*   London U.: SOAS   1976   0 7286 0028 5
Chinese Paper Cuts   *Florence Temko*   China Books & Periodicals   1982   0 835109410
Coats Book of Modern European Embroidery   *Jean Kimmond*   Batsford   1979   0 7134 3305 1
Decorative Art of Southwestern Indians   *Smith Sides*   Dover   1972   0 486 20139 2
The Decorative Arts of Sweden   *Iona Plaith*   Dover   1966   0 486 21478 8
DMC Library Series
(this is a series published by the DMC thread company giving many useful patterns and designs)
   Inca Embroideries   DMC ref 12 003–2   DMC   1978
   Chinese Embroideries   DMC ref 12 000–2   DMC   1977
   Central Asian Embroideries   DMC
   Lapland Embroideries   DMC
   Czecho-Slovakian Embroideries   DMC
Embroidery of All Russia   *M. Gostelow*   Mills & Boon   1977   0 263 06103 5

Greek Islands Embroideries   *S. L. Macmillan/Museum of Fine Arts Boston*   Tuttle, Tokyo   1978
  0 8048 1270 5
International Needlework Designs   *Mira Silverstein*   Bell & Hyman   1979   0 7135 1189 3
Islamic Art & Design 1500–1700   *J. M. Rogers*   British Museum   1983   0 7141 1428 6
Japanese Border Designs   *Theodore Menten*   Dover   1976   0 486 23180 1
Jewish Ceremonial Embroidery   *Kathryn Salomon*   Batsford   1988   0713 4 5268 4
Needlepoint Designs from Asia   *Gay Ann Rogers*   Hale   1984   0 7090 1554 2
Needlework, an Illustrated History   *Ed. Bridgeman & Drury*   Paddington Press   1978   0 7092 0045 5
Palestinian Embroidery   *S. Weir & Serene*   British Museum   1988   0 7141 1591 6
Stitches from Eastern Embroideries   *Louisa F. Pesel*   Lund, Humphries   1912
Traditional Chinese Cut-Paper Designs   *B. Melchers*   Dover   1978   0 486 23581 5
Turkish Embroidery   *Pauline Johnstone*   Van Nostrand Reinhold   1978   0 442 26799 1
Turkish Embroidery   *Gülseren Ramazanoglu*   Victoria & Albert Museum   1985   0 948107 02 2

Jacobean work–crewel embroidery

The Art of Crewel Embroidery   *Mildred Davies*   Nelson/Crown/Vista   1962/1963   0 17 140 002 X
Crewel Embroidery in England   *Joan Edwards*   Batsford/Morrow   1975   0 7134 2028 1

Lettering in embroidery

Carving Letters in Stone and Wood   *Michael Harvey*   Bodley Head   1987   0 370 31019 5
Handbook of Lettering for Embroiderers   *Elsie Svennas*   Van Nostrand   1973   0 442   28086 6
Lettering for Embroidery   *Pat Russell*   Batsford   1985   0 7134 5034 7
Lettering in Embroidery   *Janice Williams*   Batsford   1982   0 7134 3956 4
Needlework Alphabets and Designs   *Ed: Cirker*   Dover   1975   0 486 23159 3

Machine embroidery

The Creative Sewing Machine   *Anne Coleman*   Batsford   1981   0 7134 3310 8
Design for Machine Embroidery   *Ira Lillow*   Batsford   1975   0 7134 3023 0
Innovative Machine Quilting   *Hettie Risinger*   Sterling, N. Y.   1982   0 8069 7566 0
Landscape in Embroidery   *Verina Warren*   Batsford   1986   0 7134 4568 8
Machine Embroidery   *Pat Philpott*   Search Press   1979   0 85532 429 5
Machine Embroidery (Lace & Experimental Techniques)   *Moyra McNeill*   Batsford   1985
  0 7134 4485 1
Machine Embroidery: Stitch Techniques   *Valerie Campbell-Harding & Pam Watts*   Batsford   1989
  0 7134 5797 X
Machine Stitchery   *G. Swift*   Batsford   1974   0 7134 2883 X
New Designs for Machine Patchwork Embroidery   *Muriel Higgins*   Batsford   1980   0 7134 2145 2
Your Machine Embroidery   *Dorothy Benson*   Sylvan   1952

Mounting and framing

Picture Framing and Mounting   *Pamela Dick*   WI Books Ltd.   1982   0 900556 71 4

Mountmellick

see under Whitework

Patchwork

The Complete Book of Patchwork & Quilting   *Ed: Valerie Jackson*   Bell & Hyman   1985   0 7135 2577 0
Discovering Patchwork   *Richardson and Griffiths*   BBC Publications   1977   0 563 16212 0
The Log Cabin Quilt Book   *Carol Anne Wien*   Bell & Hyman   1985   0 7135 2487 1
Machine Patchwork   *Michelle Walker*   Search Press   1983   0 5532 454 6
Mitred Patchwork [Somerset]   *Margaret Wright*   Batsford   1986   0 7134 4555 6
Needlecraft 4: Patchwork   *Valerie Campbell-Harding*   Search Press   1981   0 85532 450 3
Notes on Appliqué Work and Patchwork   *Victoria & Albert Museum*   HMSO 1947
Patchwork   *Pamela Clabburn*   Batsford   1987   0 7134 5770 8
Patchwork   *Averil Colby*   Shire   1983   0 85263 631 8

Patchwork for Beginners   *Sylvia Green*   Studio Vista   1971   0 289 70091 4
Patchwork Patterns   *Jinny Beyer*   Bell & Hyman   1982   0 7135 1346 2
Seminole Patchwork   *Brandebourg*   Batsford   1983   0 7134 1320 4
Simple Patchwork   *Alice Timmins*   Batsford   1973   0 7134 2481 8
Strip Patchwork   *Valerie Campbell-Harding*   Batsford   1983   0 7134 1320 4

Quilting

A Gallery of Amish Quilts   *Robert Bishop and E. Safanda*   Phaidon/Dutton   1976   0 525 48398 5
Japanese Quilts   *Jill Liddell & Yuko Watanabe*   Dutton, Studio Vista   0 289 800 412
Notes on Appliqué Work and Patchwork   *Victoria & Albert Museum*   HMSO   1947
Notes on Quilting   *Victoria & Albert Museum*   HMSO   1949
Picture Quilts   *Joan Masters*   Bell & Hyman
Quilting   *Averil Colby*   Batsford   1987   0 7134 5901 8
Quilting: Technique, Design and Application   *Eirian Short*   Batsford   1974   0 7134 1541 X
Quilting for Today   *Moira McNeill*   Boon/Bell & Hyman   1975   0 263 05601 5
Seminole Patchwork   *Brandebourg*   Batsford   1988   0 7134 1320 4
Standard Book for Quiltmaking & Collecting   *Margaret Ickis*   Dover   1959   0 486 20582 7
Traditional Quilting   *Mavis Fitzrandolph*   Batsford   1954
The Sampler Quilt Workbook   *Dinah Travis*   Batsford   1990   0 7134 6104 7

Samplers

Sampler Making   *Joan Edwards*   Bayford   1983   0 907287 06 9
Samplers   *Averil Colby*   Batsford   1987   0 7134 4667 1
Samplers & Stitches   *Mrs Archibald (Grace) Christie*   Batsford   1934   0 7134 4796 6

Smocking

Smocking Design   *Jean Hodges*   Batsford   1987   0 7134 6344 9
Smocking in Embroidery   *Margaret Thom*   Batsford   1972   0 7134 2650 0
Smocking: Traditional & Modern Approaches   *Oenone Cave & Jean Hodges*   Batsford   1988   0 7134 5879 8
Smocks & Smocking   *Beverly Marshall*   Alpha Books   1980   0 9506171 1 3

Stumpwork

Stumpwork: Historical and Contemporary Raised Embroidery   *Muriel Best*   Batsford   1987   0 7134 5572 1
Stumpwork: The Art of Raised Embroidery   *Muriel Baker*   Bell & Hyman/Scribner   1978   0 684 15360 2

Whitework

Ayrshire Needlework   *Agnes F. Bryson*   Batsford   1989   0 7134 5928 X
Cutwork Embroidery and how to do it   *Oenone Cave*   Dover 1982   0 486 24267 6
Danish Pulled Thread Embroidery   *Handarbejdets Fremme*   Dover/Constable   1977   0 486 23474 6
Drawn Thread Embroidery   *Moyra McNeill*   Batsford   1989   07134 55977
Drawn Threadwork   *Lisa Melen (Ed: Lynette de Denne)*   Van Nostrand Reinhold   1972   0 442 78382 5
The Flowerers – The Story of Ayrshire White Needlework   *Margaret Swain*   Chambers   1955
Linen Cut Work   *Œnone Cave*   Constable/Dover   1963
Linen Embroideries   *Etta Campbell*   Batsford   1937   0 7134 6251 5
Linen for the Church   *Katherine Harris*   Embroiderers' Guild   1959
Mountmellick Work   *J Houston-Almquist*   Dolmen/Dryad Press   1985   0 85105 429 3
Needleweaving   *Edith John*   Batsford   1987   0 7134 2642 X
Pulled Thread   *Moyra McNeill*   Bell & Hyman   1986   0 7135 2668 8
Scandinavian Embroidery – Past & Present   *Edith Nielsen*   Bell & Hyman
Scottish Embroidery, Mediaeval to Modern   *Margaret Swain*   Batsford   1986   0 7134 4638 2

Journal

Embroidery   Quarterly   The Embroiderers' Guild
   Apartment 41a, Hampton Court Palace
   East Molesley, Surrey KT8 9AU England

Appendix: Diagram outlines

Using the diagram outlines

These outlines will need to be enlarged to full size before being used for the exercises in the text. As printed here, they are all reduced by 66%, so you should set the enlargement control on your photocopier to say 150% to reproduce them.

Note that not all exercises have diagrams provided.

Grid for lettering – exercise 5

Cobbler's wax
or 2B pencil

Grid for rubbings – exercise 4

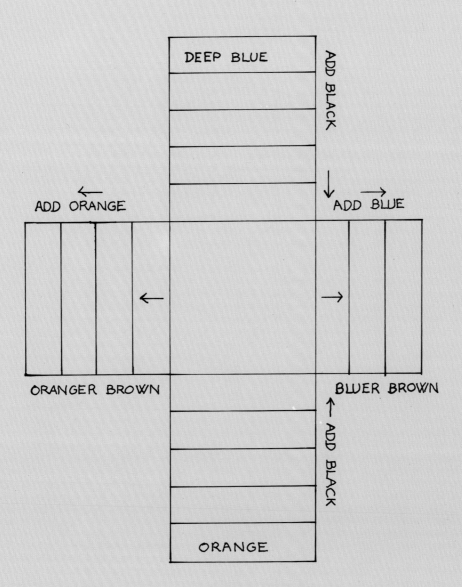

Neutral tone – exercise 8

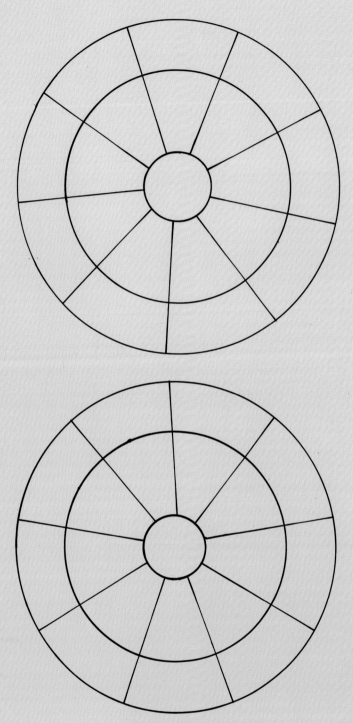

Shades and tints – exercise 11

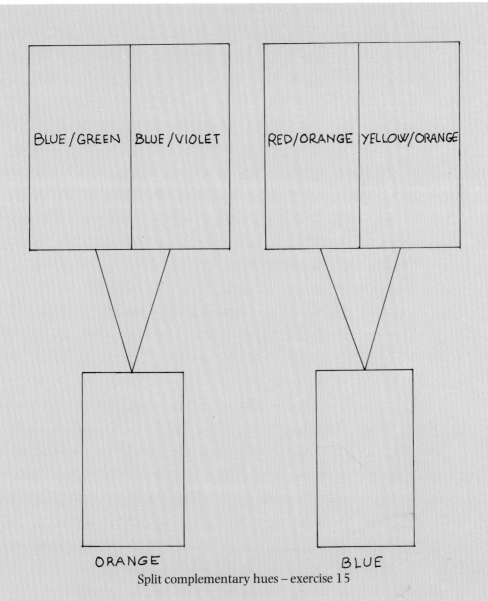

Split complementary hues – exercise 15

SEPARATIONS →

Discords and harmonies – white separation – exercise 17

HARMONY   DISCORD

Discords and harmonies – exercise 16

ORDERED SEQUENCES OF WEIGHT

REGULAR

HAPHAZARD

REVERSED

Regular, irregular and reversed sequences of weight – exercise 19

Ordered and haphazard sequences of weight – exercise 19

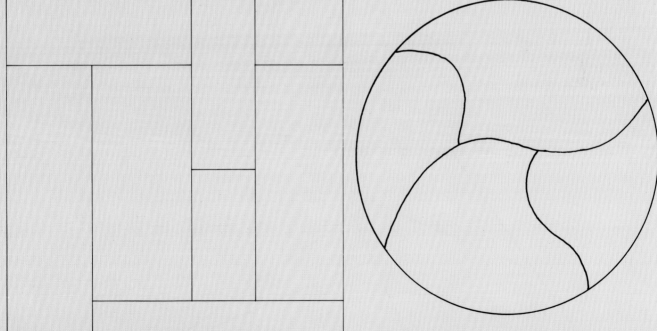

Exploding the square – exercise 21

Exploding the circle – exercise 21

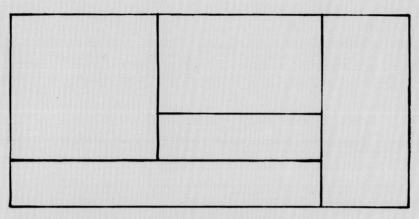

Exploding the rectangle – straight lines – exercise 21

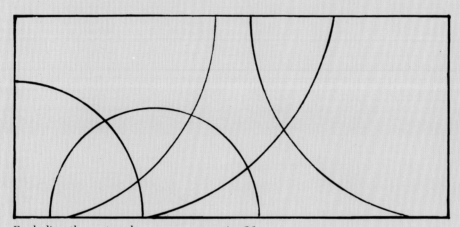

Exploding the rectangle – curves – exercise 21

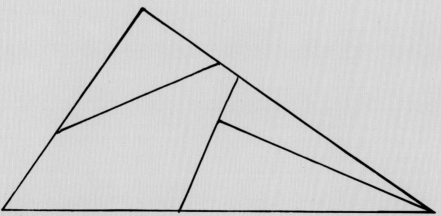

Exploding the triangle – exercise 21

Patchwork template shapes

Index

There is a separate index for Chapter 24 on page 144.

Index for Chapter 24